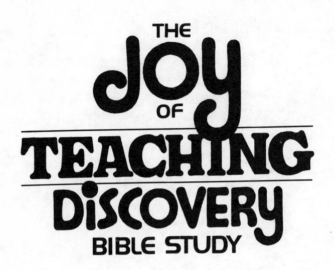

THE JOY OF TEACHING DISCOVERY BIBLE STUDY

Oletta Wald

AUGSBURG PUBLISHING HOUSE
MINNEAPOLIS, MINNESOTA

CONTENTS

INTRODUCTION

The Joy of Teaching Discovery Bible Study is a companion to my book *The Joy of Discovery in Bible Study*, in which persons are helped to become "discoverers" in Bible study and to find joy in the process. The purpose of the book is to guide persons in the basic steps in Bible study, enabling them to *observe, interpret, summarize, evaluate, apply,* and *actualize* the teachings in the Bible.

While the purpose of the first book is to help persons learn how to *study* the Bible, the purpose of this book is to help persons learn how to *teach others* to study the Bible.

Part One focuses on some of the basic principles involved in Bible teaching; Part Two provides specific instructions for helping persons develop the skills described in *The Joy of Discovery in Bible Study*.

You will note that the title of this book is not just *The Joy of Teaching,* but *The Joy of Teaching Discovery Bible Study*. The emphasis will not be on all kinds of Bible study, but on what I call "discovery Bible study." Others might call it "inductive Bible study." It is the kind of Bible study in which persons are enabled to discover the teachings in the Bible for themselves, the Bible leader serving as the guide and enabler.

This book will reflect my experiences during 20 years of working with teacher-training programs and Bible study groups, writing materials, and conducting workshops. In our teaching-training workshops, we involve persons in micro-teaching sessions in which they taught five- to fifteen-minute sessions to small groups. As one teaches, others observe. Much of the philosophy of this book has evolved through observing hundreds of these micro-teaching sessions, through the discussions with the teachers afterwards, through the sharing of how the "students" and "observers" felt about the session. I have tried to reflect in this book some basic educational principles that are true in all teaching-learning situations.

This book also reflects my most recent experiences at a Bible college in teaching courses in how to study and teach the Bible. There will be a personal quality, because most of the knowledge which I am sharing with you has come from my own experiences in teaching the Bible, writing Bible courses, and teaching others how to study and teach the Bible.

CHAPTER **1**

Discovering
the Joy in Teaching

"Teaching the Bible can be fun!"

These words came from the lips of a nineteen-year-old student who had just completed her first try at teaching a short Bible study. She had taught with a partner. They had 20 minutes to teach one section in First Peter. Their "students" had been six of their classmates. Other classmates had served as "observers," noting those things which made for effective teaching. One of the stipulations was that they had to devise methods which would enable their "students" to discover some of the teachings in the passage. They were not to lecture.

This was her first attempt at teaching the Bible on an adult basis, and she had been scared at the prospect. But her plan had worked. Her "students" had entered into an animated discussion on some of the key ideas in the passage. The "observers" had affirmed her and her partner about some of the effective elements in their lesson.

Now the ordeal was over. She was relaxing at the table where only a few minutes before she had been teaching her lesson. Everyone had gone but her, her partner, and me. As she relaxed, she again repeated, "I did not realize that teaching the Bible could be so much fun!"

I asked her what she meant by fun.

"It was such fun," she answered, "to see the eyes of the students light up and their faces break into smiles as they discovered some of the things we had discovered in our study."

In this first attempt she had discovered the *joy of teaching discovery Bible study.* While there are a variety of joys a teacher might experience, there is a special thrill in seeing the "lights" go on in students' eyes as they begin to discover some things for themselves in a passage of Scripture.

Now it is true that not all teaching is a joy. Sometimes teaching can be frustrating and discouraging. Many have tried being a teacher and have found it so discouraging that they quit.

5

One of the paradoxes of teaching is that it can be both satisfying and frustrating, depending on circumstances, responses of the students, the kind of teacher preparation, and methods used. Teaching has the potentials for both agonies and ecstasies. Any veteran teacher knows that no session plan is foolproof. What will work with one group may not work at all with another.

One of the purposes of this book is to analyze teaching and focus on those things which have proved to be the most effective in teaching-learning situations.

Approaches to Bible Study

There are two general approaches to conducting a Bible study: the "telling approach" and the "discovery approach." Most teachers will operate under one approach or the other; some teachers use a mixture of both.

The Telling Approach

In this approach the teacher mainly lectures. You "tell" your students what is contained in a passage. You might use visual and audio aids, but for the most part you view your learners as "listeners." You are the authority. You have become the "discoverer" and you share your discoveries with your learners. They are the "receivers," and you are the "giver."

Many teachers feel most comfortable with this approach. It is not so risky! You need only to think about what you will bring to your learners. You do not have to worry about their responses—which might be upsetting to your plan and even to your interpretation of a passage.

Many persons feel that it is the best way to teach the Bible because it is the "easiest way to get things across to your learners."

The Discovery Approach

In this approach your focus is not so much on yourself as on your students. Your foremost desire is to enable them to become "discoverers." In preparing for this kind of study, your concern will not be just on *what* to teach, but also on *how* to enable your learners to discover the teachings in a Bible passage. Your concern will be not only to help them discover what you have discovered, but to help them go beyond you. No longer will you come as the expert, but you come also as a learner, desiring that you and your learners might become "discoverers" together.

This does not mean that you may not do some "telling." If you have done some serious studying before the class, you will have more insights than your students may have, especially if they do not do much homework. Your primary aim will be to enable them to discover what they can. Then you will try to enrich the study with additional insights. If your students do some previous study before class, you may be amazed at the many insights they have which you may not have discovered. In "discovery" Bible study, you will find that you also will be enriched by what your students have discovered.

Why Discovery Bible Study?

Possibly you are asking, "Why this emphasis on discovery Bible study? What is so valuable about this approach?" Consider the following statement by William Barclay:

"It is only when truth is discovered
    that it is appropriated.
When a man is simply told the truth,
    it remains external to him
    and he can quite easily forget it.
When he is led to discover the truth himself,
    it becomes an integral part of him
    and he never forgets."

Note the key words in this passage: *discover, appropriated, truth, external, integral, forgets.* Think seriously about the reality of this statement in your own life, the times you have been led to discover something which you never forgot.

This is especially true in Bible study. Everyone knows that we who teach get the most out of a Bible study. After we have put in many hours studying a passage, discovering some of its basic teachings, we may never forget the passage.

The tragedy is that we teachers have often denied this same privilege to our students. We come to our Bible classes *loaded* with all kinds of Bible "goodies" and try to feed our students as much as we have time for. We deny them the joy of discovery by telling them everything *we* have discovered.

One of the reasons that persons quickly forget what they are told has to do with the way we learn. We are told that we remember about 10 percent of what we hear, 50 percent of what we see, 75 percent of what we say, and 90 percent of what we do. Thus we can see that if the Bible teacher does all the talking and the students only listen, they may not remember much of what they hear, unless some of the other activities of learning are included.

Reactions to Discovery Bible Study

The best criteria for discovery Bible study is the reactions of the students themselves. While you will always have some who prefer to have the teacher do all the telling, the majority appreciate learning the skills in Bible study. They want to become "discoverers" them-

7

selves. As you help persons become discovers, you will begin to experience some of these joys . . .

- the joy of watching faces brighten as they discover truths in the Bible;
- the joy of hearing students share observations which you have not seen;
- the joy of observing small groups so engrossed in their discussion that they do not want to quit;
- the joy of enabling persons to develop their creative potentials;
- the joy of knowing that you are helping persons develop skills which they can use in all study;
- the joy of hearing persons say . . .

    "Now I know how to approach the scriptures."
    "I had such fun studying that I did not want to stop."
    "No longer do I feel frustrated or defeated in study."
    "Now I am ready to go to college; I know how to study."
    "The skills I have learned have revolutionized my Bible study."
    "I have been helped to value my mind and its potentials."
    "The more I have learned how to study the Bible, the more I enjoy studying the Bible and the more real Christ has become to me."

CHAPTER 2

Equipping the Saints

Before we begin to focus on the specifics in Bible teaching, we should consider the most basic questions: Why study the Bible? Why involve persons in Bible study? Why be concerned about their becoming *discoverers* and *rememberers?*

We have been living in an era when the Bible has been "up for grabs." Persons have doubted its validity in the curriculum of a church. It has been condemned as old-fashioned, irrelevant, no longer speaking to the problems of our day. But our problems today have become so complicated and frightening and man seems so helpless in trying to solve them, that more and more persons are turning again to the Bible. Down through the years it outlasts all of its enemies and even survives some of its overly zealous friends. Could it be what it claims to be, the eternal Word of God with an integrity that speaks to the need of every age?

Why Study the Bible?

I believe that the Bible itself gives the clearest reason for studying it. We read in 2 Timothy 3:14-17:

> *But as for you, continue in what you have learned and have firmly believed, knowing from whom you learned it and how from childhood you have been acquainted with the sacred writings which are able to instruct you for salvation through faith in Christ Jesus. All scripture is inspired by God and profitable for teaching, for reproof, for correction, and for training in righteousness, that the man of God may be complete, equipped for every good work.*

One of the key words in the passage is *equipped.* The writer of 2 Timothy says that scripture is able to equip the man of God for every good work. This same emphasis on equipping is also found in Ephesians 4:11-13.

> *And his gifts were that some should be apostles, some prophets, some evangelists, some pastors and teachers, to equip the saints for the work of*

ministry, for building up the body of Christ, until we all attain to the unity of the faith and of the knowledge of the Son of God, to mature manhood, to the measure of the stature of the fulness of Christ.

The Greek term for equip is *katartismon*, a word used for the setting of broken bones, putting joints in place, for mending of nets, for bringing together opposing factions.

The picture in this passage in Ephesians is that the leaders in the church were to equip the saints for the work of ministry. To do this, the leaders were to educate, guide, and help the members of the body of Christ so that they might "mend" the broken lives in the world in which they lived. The aim of the leaders was to help build up the whole body of Christ until all the members came to a oneness of faith and knowledge of our Lord Jesus Christ.

In many of our churches today members are being asked to become "ministers" to each other and to the world about them without being equipped. One of the primary purposes of a congregation should be to equip its members to become "healers" in a world full of hurts and suffering.

When teaching this passage in Ephesians, I have asked persons to name some of the areas in their lives in which they need to be equipped if they are to serve as "ministers," persons who serve others in the world. They have listed some of the following areas:

- Certainty of their own relationship with Christ
- Knowledge about biblical truths as basis for their faith
- Insight into their own selves and personal needs
- Understanding how to establish positive personal relationships
- Skills in vocalizing and sharing their faith
- Sensitivity to the needs of others
- Fellowship for personal strength and encouragement
- Identification of their own gifts
- Practical helps in being a "minister"

Ways to Equip Through Bible Study

As we think about equipping persons for ministry, we need to consider the dimensions in Bible study and Bible teaching: the *vertical dimension* and the *horizontal dimension*. As teachers we are all aware of the vertical and horizontal dimensions emphasized in the Bible, but possibly we have not thought of them in terms of Bible teaching as well. Yet if we are concerned about equipping persons, we need to be conscious of their potentials in both study and teaching.

Vertical Dimension

The vertical dimension in the Bible focuses on God's relationship with man: God's revelation of himself through his Word, especially through Jesus Christ as the Living Word; and man's response to this revelation of Jesus Christ through faith and love. This is the primary emphasis in the Bible and is the main purpose for studying and teaching the Bible. Most Bible teachers seek to enable their students to grow in "the grace and knowledge of the Lord Jesus Christ." This is an important dimension in the equipping of the saints.

In most congregations there are many persons who do not have the certainty of their relationship with Jesus Christ. While they may have the "head" knowledge, they do not have the "heart" knowledge, that inner assurance of peace with God. Some may not want too close a fellowship with Christ and have not made a personal commitment to him. Still there are others who are sincere in their faith, but have not been able to appropriate all that is theirs through the finished work of Christ. Through Bible study, many people have come to a conscious personal faith in Christ, experiencing his joy and peace as they claimed God's promises in his Word.

As to knowledge of Christian beliefs, ignorance is not bliss in the Christian life. In fact, if you continue to study this passage in Ephesians 4, you will find that Paul states that one of the reasons Christians need to grow in "the knowledge of the Son of God" is so that they "may no longer be as children tossed to and fro by every wind of doctrine." Unless a person has a biblical basis for his faith, he is at the mercy of "the cunning of men." The better a person knows his Bible, the better able he is to give reasons for his Christian faith.

Horizontal Dimension

The Bible also emphasizes the *horizontal* dimension: man's relationship to man. As persons grow in their understanding and experience of God's love in their own lives, they are to express this love in their relationships with others. The two dimensions of Bible study are expressed in the two commandments: "You shall love the Lord your God with all your heart, and with all your soul, and with all your strength, and with all your mind; and your neighbor as yourself."

This dimension is also emphasized in Bible studies. As teachers, we desire that our students will reflect Christ's love in their relationships with other people.

Importance of Both Dimensions

While we as Bible teachers may claim to be concerned about both dimensions, we do not always reflect our concern in the way we teach. If we are truly interested in equipping our people in as many areas as possible, we need to emphasize the two dimensions in both words and opportunities. If we only lecture, we are involving them in a one-dimensional study. We are providing opportunity for them to respond only vertically. In their hearts and minds they can respond to God as he speaks to them through his Word. While they may respond intellectually concerning horizontal relationships, in the context of lecture, they have no opportunity to respond actually. Only as we also involve them in sharing and relating to the others in their study group, do we provide the second dimension, the horizontal opportunities.

Possibly you are asking why the emphasis on both dimensions. Is not the vertical one enough? We need both if persons are to be effectively equipped for growth in their Christian lives and in becoming "ministers" in the world about them. For many persons the quality of their horizontal relationship is the significant factor which enables them to grow in their vertical relationship with the Lord. Until persons feel they are loved and accepted by others, they sometimes have difficulty believing that they are loved and accepted by God.

The more persons are enabled to relate to each other in a small group as they focus on the truths in God's Word, the greater is the potential for them to become equipped in these many areas: in believing in the forgiving love of God; in gaining insight into themselves and their own needs; in learning how to relate to others; in finding personal strength and encouragement; in identifying their gifts and potentials; in developing concern for the needs of others; in verbalizing their faith.

Let us consider the last of these needs in the list, the need for learning how to verbalize our Christian faith. It may seem strange to list this as a need, but verbalizing our Christian faith is of more significance than many of us realize. Sara Little has expressed this truth in these words:

"Somehow the nature of the biblical witness seems to be such that a person must become involved himself, must put forth effort to understand, if he is to appropriate the biblical faith. There is a sense in which a person cannot appropriate unless he can articulate its meaning. This may be one of the reasons why participation is desirable and why insights and discoveries become both possessions and determining forces more definitely when they are verbalized.

"Therefore, it is important that the church make it possible for persons to witness to one another about their understanding of the meaning of the biblical revelation for particular situations, not legalistically or in judgment, but as neighbors and friends to one another, bound together within the *koinonia*."

Personal Convictions About Bible Study

My primary reason for promoting Bible study has to do with what the Bible has done for my own personal life.

While I had been a confessing Christian for many years, I was in my thirties before I became involved in the systematic Bible study which became so meaningful in my life. Before then I had been involved in a kind of hit-and-miss variety. It was when I attended a Bible school that I experienced the tremendous value of Bible study. As I became involved in concentrated Bible study, I became aware of the emptiness and hunger of my soul and of the uncertainties in my life, the uncertainty of my relationship with God, the uncertainty of my relationship with others and with self.

As I continued in my studies, I had the sensation of my inner self being clothed with flesh. I began to experience a certainty in my relationship with God, a certainty that man could not give me, but that the Holy Spirit did give me through his Word. My entire life took on a new dimension. I found Bible study gave me strength for my daily living, new direction for my life, a new understanding of myself and my relationship with others.

I did not "believe" differently, but I learned how to claim the promises of God and how to appropriate what God offered me in Jesus Christ. I began to experience the guiding, strengthening, sustaining, and comforting power of God through his Word. I found a peace and a joy which I never knew before. Jeremiah's words became real to me: "Thy words were found and I did eat them, and thy words became a joy and delight of my heart." Bible study became a delight to the heart! Jer 15:16

Because of the joy and power I had experienced through the study of the Bible, I became interested in involving others in Bible study, wishing that they too might experience the blessing which Bible study can bring. While I was grateful for my opportunity to attend a Bible school and wished all persons could have the opportunity, I was realistic enough to know that was impossible. The major Bible study emphasis had to be in the congregations. I knew that congregations varied in their Bible study emphases. Some had very active Bible study classes and some had very few. I also realized that many pastors tried to involve their members in Bible studies but the members themselves seemed to be indifferent.

One of my reasons for promoting Bible study was my conviction that Bible study was important to growth in one's personal Christian life. I felt that we had many "powerless" persons in our congregations who were "empty of soul" like myself, persons who did not know the joy and the peace one could have in their relationship with God. The result was that they were not very active in the congregation or in the Lord's work.

While I encouraged Bible studies as much as possible, I also knew that Bible studies in themselves did not always create new life in persons. I knew that it was the way the Bible study was taught that determined the degree in which it was an influence in a person's life.

Bible study was not like taking some medicine—if we could just swallow it, it would have value in our lives. Some Bible studies were so poorly taught that I wondered about their value.

I grieved when I heard women say, "I quit the women's meeting. All they did was study the Bible and it was so dull. I did not want to waste my time any more at such a meeting." While I grieved, I could not fault the persons. I too had attended some of these dull studies.

I remember being invited to speak at women's meetings. Before my speech, someone would conduct a Bible study. Sometimes I had a feeling that they had the Bible study out of duty: "You ought to have Bible study at a church meeting." The leader would read out of the leader's guide. Most of the persons would not have a Bible with them, but it really did not matter. The leader seldom referred to the Bible anyway. We all sat and patiently "listened" until it was over. I wanted to weep as I sat and listened to the reading. What I was witnessing was worse than no Bible study at all. People were being thoroughly convinced that studying the Bible was dull and uninteresting . . . and at best only something which a person endured. No wonder countless persons were convinced that Bible study was boring. I grieved for the leader as well because she knew no better way to conduct the study.

I determined that I would do all I could to help persons realize that Bible study could be interesting and exciting. I developed a consuming desire to help persons discover the joy that could be theirs in studying the Bible. As I conducted Bible studies, I found that the more I involved them in the discovery process, the greater was their interest in the study. So through the years I have continued to experiment, but I knew that my task was twofold: to learn how to conduct effective Bible studies and how to enable others to conduct effective Bible studies.

I have this yearning to help persons discover the joy in studying the Word because I believe that in that context they will also discover its dynamic power in their own personal lives, as a foundation for their faith, as strength for their daily living, as direction in ministry. Most of all I believe that as they find joy in studying God's Word they will also discover the joy and peace that can be theirs in the living Word, Jesus Christ.

These yearnings and hopes have been the foundation for all that I have included in this book. My prayer is that through some of the suggestions in this book you who teach will find greater satisfaction in your teaching as you enable others to find satisfaction in their study of the Bible.

CHAPTER 3

Preparing for Teaching

There are three general areas which you as a teacher must consider when thinking of conducting a Bible study. 1) your own personal study; 2) your preparation of a session plan; 3) your participation in the teaching session itself.

Personal Study

In the book, *The Joy of Discovery in Bible Study*, I have described in detail the steps a person should follow in order to gain insight in a Bible passage. These steps are briefly reviewed in this chapter. While you might not follow the exact order, in one way or another you will have to consider all of the steps in order to understand a passage.

1. OBSERVE the details in a passage.

This has to be step one because you cannot interpret or apply a passage until you have observed its details. The more carefully you observe the details, the better you will know what are its major points and what to focus on in your teaching session. When observing a passage, look for these things: key words, admonitions, contrasts, comparisons, illustrations, repetitions, progression of ideas, cause and effect relations, promises, grammatical constructions, atmosphere, important connectives, literary form, general structure of passage. Diagramming and charting can also be aids to observing the details in a passage and its key ideas.

2. INTERPRET the teachings.

While you are observing the details in a passage, you should also be asking yourself *questions for understanding:* "Why is the author saying what he is saying? What does he mean by this word or statement? What is the significance—what is the implication—of these words and statements?" These are just examples of the kinds of questions you might be asking. The asking of questions is the bridge between observation and interpretation. The purpose is to stir your thinking about the key ideas and to point out what needs to be interpreted.

After you have carefully observed the details in a passage and asked yourself questions about some of the key ideas, you are ready to interpret the key ideas. You will gain insight into meaning by doing these things:

- define words through use of dictionary
- compare translations
- look up cross references
- consult other resources
- wrestle with meanings

We include wrestling as one of the means for gaining insight into a passage. After defining words, comparing translations, studying cross references and other resources, you will need to evaluate, discern, wrestle with the insights gained in order to come to your own conclusions.

3. SUMMARIZE key teachings.

While summarizing is listed as Step 3, it really is a process which should be done in connection with both observation and interpretation. You should try to summarize the facts you observe and then the meaning of the facts.

4. EVALUATE fairly what the author has written.

Not until you have a clear concept of what the author is trying to say and what he meant by what he wrote can you honestly judge the validity of the passage. Thus evaluation must come after observation and interpretation. When evaluating a passage, one must be fair to the writer of the book. Too often persons evaluate Scripture according to their own private prejudices, emotions, and present-day culture.

5. APPLY and ACTUALIZE the teachings.

While application and actualization are listed last in the study, this does not mean they are last in importance. Application is the fruit which will come forth through the other processes. Application is a growing process, not superimposed in a superficial way, but rising out of all the other processes.

Some General Reminders

While we all will agree that our own personal study is very important in the teaching process, this is an area which we often short-cut because we feel we don't have time to do what we should. Indeed there are shortcuts you can make in personal study, but the kind of effort you put into your personal study does in a great measure determine the effectiveness of your session.

If you have not used the *Joy of Discovery in Bible Study* as a guide for studying a Bible passage, I suggest you do so before you try to follow any of the suggestions in this book. As has been said, this chapter is a summary of the skills described in the book.

Formulation of a Session Plan

After you have made a thorough study of the passage you are to teach, your next task is to formulate your session plan. When planning a session, there are definite areas of concern to consider. We shall list them in this chapter and describe them in more detail in other chapters.

1. TEACHER. Because you are the key to an effective session you have to begin with yourself. You will have to decide what roles as a teacher you see yourself assuming in the teaching of the session.

2. LEARNER. Your next area of concern has to do with your learners. As you plan your session, you need to take into consideration who they are, what are their interests, abilities, needs, and background.

3. CONCEPTS (BIG IDEAS). Your third area of concern has to do with the focus of your session. What are the concepts—the key ideas which you plan to focus on? You cannot emphasize all of the ideas in a passage. You will need to select those which you think are the most relevant in understanding the passage.

4. OBJECTIVES. An objective is a statement of purpose or goal in terms of what the learners are to accomplish. You need to determine how you want your learners to respond to the teachings in the passage. What do you hope your learners will know, feel, or be able to do that they were not able to feel, know, or do before the lesson?

5. PROCESS. After you have determined your concepts and objectives, then you need to decide what kind of activities you might involve your learners so that your objectives will be accomplished. Process has to do with activities, materials, resources, and organization of the lesson.

6. LEARNER RESPONSE. While we all are hopeful that our learners will respond positively to the session activities, seldom do we consciously formulate possible responses. I am encouraging you to think about possible responses you hope to get from your learners. This means that as you list activities in your plan, you might also

list possible ways you can anticipate your learners' response to the activities. The purpose is to enable you to identify some clues to measure how your objectives are being accomplished.

7. TIME-SITUATION. All planning is limited by the two factors of time and teaching situation. Outside forces often control both the time and our teaching situations. While sometimes we can improve our situations by moving around furniture, we are usually stuck with the time. So we have to plan a session that can be accomplished in the time allotment.

Involvement in Teaching the Session

The third major area for consideration has to do with your involvement in the teaching session itself. I do not like to call it the "presentation of a lesson," because that implies the teacher doing everything. If you are interested in learning how to conduct a "discovery Bible study" you will not be "presenting a lesson." You will be involving your students in a variety of activities through which they might discover the truths in a passage themselves.

This area also will be discussed in greater detail in a later chapter. In this chapter we have just tried to give you an overview of all the areas in which a teacher must involve himself when teaching the Bible. Let us review them again:

- Personal study of the passage
- Formulation of the session plan
- Involvement in teaching the session.

CHAPTER 4

Identifying Your Teaching Role

No doubt you have purchased this book because you are interested in teaching. Possibly you have been a Bible teacher for many years and are interested in learning new ways to increase your effectiveness as a teacher. Others of you may have tried to teach and found the experience very discouraging. Your hope is that this book might enable you to find some satisfaction in teaching.

Books on teaching often emphasize the characteristics teachers should have. We are told that to be effective teachers we must be enthusiastic, energetic, patient, loving, friendly, understanding, dedicated, committed Christians, etc. We are not denying that these characteristics are important but sometimes the listing of them is more depressing than helpful. We feel loaded with guilt because we know we cannot measure up to the list. Rather than concentrating on characteristics, let us think of ourselves as unique persons with many potentials which we hope to develop in our teaching efforts.

While we all are unique and do not have to be like any one else in our teaching, we all assume many roles. Personality traits and roles are not the same. A *personality trait* is an attitude or quality a teacher may have such as kindness, enthusiasm, patience, etc. A *role* is a stance or pattern of behavior that a teacher assumes in performing his task as a teacher, even as parents must assume many roles to function as parents. Roles have to do with self-image and teacher behavior. The image a teacher has of himself and his role often determines what he does and how he functions as a teacher. Let me describe some common roles.

Information Giver

I list this role first because it is probably the most common role we assume as Bible teachers. Many persons refuse to teach the Bible because they feel they know too little about the Bible, they have too little *information* to give. When we view our role as *information givers,* we view our students as *receivers,* and we will mainly lecture. If we have done some serious study before the class period, we will have many things we want to share with our students. Traditionally, the view of the Bible teacher in a congregation was that she or he should be the expert in knowledge about the Bible. Because so few thought of themselves as *the expert,* most congregations have had very few persons who would volunteer to be the Bible teacher. In many congregations there might be only one or two persons who feel they "qualify" as the Bible teacher.

Inspirer

Another common role to assume as a Bible teacher is that of being an *inspirer,* one who should inspire persons to commit their lives to Christ, to live a more dedicated Christian life, etc. As the inspirer we see our role as one to arouse positive feelings, to stimulate, to motivate, to lift the sights of our students. Usually as the inspirer we see our role as the *giver* and our students as the *recipients.* We recognize that the Holy Spirit is *the* Inspirer, but we see ourselves as the vehicle through whom the Holy Spirit works.

Challenger

Possibly this role is not too different from the *inspirer* except in intensity. As inspirers we think of helping persons feel positively toward the teachings in a passage. Whereas as *challengers* we seek to challenge persons to make decisions. Our concern is that our students "actualize" the truths in a passage. We want our students to do more than just study. We want them to carry out the biblical challenges in their own lives. We are decision oriented.

Enabler

All of the above roles are more or less teacher-centered. We view ourselves in the role of the aggressor. We concentrate on what *we* might cause to happen in a class. We view ourselves mainly in the role of the *giver* and our students in the roles of the *receivers.*

The role of the *enabler* is an entirely different role. No longer is the focus on ourselves, but mainly on our students. We view them not so much as *receivers* but as *doers.* Instead of seeing ourselves in the role of the *giver,* sharing with our students our discoveries, we seek to devise ways to help them become *discoverers.*

To *enable* means to call forth, to allow to emerge, to help someone realize his potential. To be an *enabler* means to call forth the best in each member of a group, to enable him to share his ideas, his hopes, his dreams, his concerns, to help him realize his potentials. No longer do we view our students as *receivers* but as *doers.*

While we may still seek to inspire and challenge our students, as an enabler we know that we cannot use the lecture as our main method.

We have to devise all kinds of ways to enable our students to learn to become discoverers.

Stimulator, Facilitator, Guide, Catalyst

These roles are closely related to the enabler. As an enabler we will have to be the stimulator, the facilitator, the guide, the catalyst at different times. Our students may come to us with the mind-set that they cannot become discoverers. They may be so used to having others do their thinking, that they may not want to struggle with thinking themselves. So we as the leaders have to devise ways to motivate, stimulate, and facilitate so that they can realize their potentials.

Encourager, Affirmer

Most persons have a very poor self-image as far as their ability to study the Bible. If they have never done much studying on their own, if they are used to being spoon-fed, they may be thoroughly convinced that they cannot become discoverers. In fact some may like best for the leader to continue to be their discoverer.

On the other hand, there will be those who are tired of being "fed." They want to learn to do their own "chewing." Even so, if we are to help persons to become discoverers, they are in need of lots of encouragement and affirmation. We must involve them in activities in which they have a measure of satisfaction all along. They have to be assured that what they are doing is OK. They are apt to think of their own discoveries in terms of "right and wrong": Are the things I am discovering in a passage "right" or "wrong"? We have to help them think in terms of "learning," what did I learn in the study of the passage? They need help to measure their learning by degrees from a little insight to greater insight. This takes lots of encouragement on the part of the teacher.

Learner

Think of yourself as a *learner* along with your students. Teaching is a "becoming" process. No one arrives. Be willing to experiment, take risks, make mistakes in order to learn. Often it is through our failures and mistakes that we learn the most about teaching.

When something does not work, be honest with your students and admit your problems. Invite them to analyze the teaching situation. Don't feel that you must have the solution to all problems or know all the answers. Identify with your students' problems. Let them know that teachers also are human with doubts, frustrations, and struggles. They will respect you for your honesty. Also share with them your dependency on God and the way you have found him as your guide and source of strength.

Some teachers have never thought of the role of a *learner* as an important one in teaching. When we go into a class assuming the role of the expert, we immediately place ourselves in a difficult position. Most of us in local congregations are not experts in our knowledge of the Bible. To be thought of as an expert is frightening because we know we cannot measure up to that role. If we try to live up to that role, we find ourselves in a precarious position. In order to save our face, we become rigid in our teaching. The only way we can convince others that we are the expert is not to allow them to have a viewpoint. Our views must be the right ones. This can create conflicts because no one can claim to be THE expert. No one knows all the answers to the teachings in the Bible, not even the learned Bible scholars.

It is much easier to come to a Bible class as a *learner* along with the other learners. Indeed, we should come with more knowledge than our students. They have a right to expect us to put in more study than they. Even so, we can come realizing that we too are learners and that we can learn from our students. This kind of an attitude creates a much better relationship between student and teacher. Students will respect us more as *learners* than they might respect us as the *experts*. Coming as a learner takes off our shoulders the burden of having to be the expert.

We should view ourselves as learners not only in terms of our students, but also in terms of our session plan. Even though we consider ourselves as learners, we still plan very carefully what to do in the class session. But we view every session as a learning session in terms of teaching as well as in terms of the insights into a passage. Not all of our plans will work, but no session need to be considered a total failure. We can learn as much from our "failures" and mistakes as we can from our successes. After each session, we should ask ourselves, "What did I learn about teaching today?"

Coming into a session as a learner relieves one of the burdens of being the "perfect" teacher and having the "perfect" session. We can view any session in a relaxed way, looking forward to it as a learning experience for both us and our students.

Remember that a teacher always needs a *barrel* and a *basket*. Into the barrel we place those things which worked in a session. Into the basket we throw the things that did not work.

Resource

To view yourself as a *resource* is different from viewing yourself as an *information giver*. As a resource, we still view ourselves in the role of the *enabler*. We know that our students may not put in as much time studying the lesson as we do and they will not have the information we may have. In our teaching, we encourage them to share the insights they do have, and then we add to what they say. Our role is to enrich what they give. We should have the answers to the more difficult passages in the Bible.

As the *resource,* we also direct students where they might find answers to some of their questions. While students may not want us to do their thinking for them, they do appreciate it if we know more than they and can fill in the gaps. They want us to know more than they, but they really do not want us to give them the "whole load of hay," especially when they have a little "hay" they too want to share!

Example

This is not so much a *role* a teacher assumes as *who he or she is.* There is no doubt that what a person is has more influence than all of the roles he assumes. I know that when we think of ourselves as the example, we think that we should be that *perfect* example. Again we feel troubled because we are so conscious of our inadequacies. The kind of example which persons can most easily identify with is the teacher who quits pretending he is the perfect person, and admits that he too is human with struggles, doubts, hang-ups, fears. As we share with them our struggles, so we share with them our source of help and strength, Jesus Christ and his power. As we see ourselves as "ministers" to our students, let us also allow them to "minister" to us.

CHAPTER 5

Knowing Your Learners

A teacher's first concern is usually about himself: Who am I to be a teacher? Do I know enough? Will I be any good at teaching?

Our next concern has to be our learners: Who are they? What are they like? What are their interests, needs, concerns, background?

You can have all kinds of learners in your class—the young and the old, the educated and the non-educated, those with a strong Christian background and those with little or none, the mature Christians and the very new, the seekers and even the antagonists.

Each learner is unique. Each brings with him his interests, needs, background, hang-ups, feelings, experiences, which have conditioned him to think and respond in his own ways. He brings with him a set of attitudes toward religion, toward culture, toward social groups, toward politics and economic policies which he has learned from his family, his community, his church, and his culture. And these attitudes are not changed very quickly.

While all learners are different in background, abilities and potentials, yet they have much in common.

Concerned About Himself

Even as the teacher is concerned about himself, so the learner is concerned about himself. He will attend your class for what he can get out of it for his own needs. This is true whether he is nine or ninety. He comes with his problems, interests, needs, concerns, questions, and yearnings, and he hopes that in some way you will meet some of these needs. He may not know what his needs are or even what he wants, but the more you are meeting his needs, the more he will positively respond to the class. This does not mean that we as teachers try to find out everyone's needs and start there, but it means that we should be responsive to the learner's concern about himself.

Embarrassed by Lack of Knowledge

Many of your learners may not have an extensive knowledge about the Bible. Because of this lack of knowledge, some people will be hesitant in sharing for fear of revealing their lack.

When teaching the Bible, it is important to try to discover in some way how much your students know about the Bible. You have to do this rather cautiously, because you will try not to embarrass them. Some may know so little that they have difficulty even finding books in the Bible. When you direct your students to locate a reference, give a clue as to where it is.

Responds Both Intellectually and Emotionally

While you may be conscious of only his intellectual response by what he is saying, we must remember he is responding emotionally as well. He has feelings about what is being taught. If his feelings are positive, he is more apt to respond positively to what is taught. If his feelings are negative, he may reject what is taught. His feelings may control his responses more than his intellect.

Is a Decision Maker

No matter what kind of experiences you involve your learners in—reading, discussing, listening, exploring, observing, expressing—they are also making decisions. They are accepting or rejecting, believing or disbelieving, liking or disliking what is being taught. As we have already said, their decisions are more apt to be related to their feelings than to their intellect. Decisions are affected by the following:

- feelings toward the teacher and members of group,
- sense of belonging in the group,
- the degree of involvement in the lesson,
- the way needs are being met.

Desires Satisfaction and Achievement

Every person wants to have a sense of satisfaction and achievement in what he does. There is a strong inherent desire in all persons to learn, to gain knowledge, to solve problems, to develop skills, to discover, explore, or experiment. No matter what he is involved in, the learner wants a sense of accomplishment, a feeling that he is achieving something.

This is as true in a Bible study as in other areas. Students want the sense of learning something they did not know before. If a student is confused or frustrated, or if he feels the study is repetitive of what he already knew, he will become disinterested.

Comes with Many Problems

While a few of your learners may be "problem free," the majority will come to your class burdened with many problems. Wearing the mask of cheerfulness, they will seek to hide their inner hurts. They may be having problems with feeling inadequate, lonely, rejected, or bitter. They may be carrying a load of guilt for past mistakes and failures. They may be equally burdened with "ought-to's"—"I ought to be doing more than I am"—"I ought to be a better Christian than I am"—"I ought not to be like I am." They may be self-condemning, unable to forgive themselves or like themselves.

Our learner may also be having problems with others. He may be on the verge of a divorce, worried about the actions of his children, living or working with a difficult person, taking care of a dear one that is dying of cancer, concerned about financial problems.

He may even be having problems with God. He may be uncertain about his relationship with him, may be angry at him because he feels that the Lord has treated him unjustly. He may blame God for some of his difficulties. He may be searching and longing for peace with God. He tries to be a "good Christian," but somehow things don't work for him. He prays, but is uncertain that the Lord always hears him.

Needs the Good News

While no one will have all the problems mentioned in the previous section, everyone has experienced some of them. All are in need of the Good News that Jesus Christ is for the lost, the lonely, the guilty, the discouraged, the hurting. You will have some in your class who have experienced the Good News of forgiveness of sins, of release from the bondages of sin and guilt and self-condemnation. They are rejoicing in the Lord's love and peace and grace.

You will find that the majority yearn for a closer relationship with the Lord. While we who teach may be very concerned about doctrines and "correct" teachings, our students are more concerned about the reality of a relationship. Through our teaching we can help some lay hold on all that can be theirs in Christ, but others are so locked within themselves, they have difficulty being open to the Lord. They need a small, loving fellowship group in which they can open themselves to others. As they learn to share their feelings and fears with others and experience their love and acceptance, they can open themselves to the Lord and claim his love and acceptance.

CHAPTER 6

Selecting Your Focus

Identifying the Key Ideas

One of your first tasks in planning a Bible session is to decide *what* you will teach and *why*. If you have made a thorough study of a passage, you will have much information and many insights to convey to your students. In fact, one of the problems which most Bible teachers face is that they have more material than there is time to discuss. The teacher always faces the problem of selecting what to emphasize. There are several approaches to make when considering what to emphasize.

Verse-by-verse Approach

You may decide to approach a passage verse by verse. You really do not make a selection, but expound on the verses in logical order and cover as many as time allows. This is the approach we find in some religious radio programs. The disadvantage of this kind of teaching is that persons may get insights into the particulars, but never a feeling for the whole passage.

The Story Approach

If your Bible study centers on one of the Gospels or Old Testament books, then your approach might be story by story. Your aim then would be to teach the contents of each story. This is often the approach used with children. But even though you focus mainly on the facts in a story, you consciously or unconsciously teach more than facts. Most of the stories contain inherent truths which are reflected in the actions of the characters. The stories included in the Bible have a single purpose, to tell how God revealed himself to man and how man responded to God. They are not just stories but are there to tell *the* story of God's plan of salvation for his world. Therefore, just focusing on the *facts* in a story is not enough. You need also to focus on the truths imbedded in the story. This does not mean moralizing the truths in the story, but highlighting them.

The Concept Approach

Whether a Bible passage is narrative, discourse, poetic, or parabolic, all have one thing in common. All have some key concepts, key ideas which need to be discovered in our personal study and emphasized in our teaching. We need to remember that we are not just teaching verses or paragraphs or stories, but we are teaching the key ideas, the key concepts in the verse or paragraph or story.

We use the term *concept* in a broad way. The dictionary defines the concept as a *thought, an opinion, mental image* of a thing formed through experiences. We might also define a concept as an *idea, understanding, insight.*

The Bible contains many concepts, but the majority of them are:

- Concepts about God—Father, Son and Holy Spirit
- Concepts about man's relationship with God
- Concepts about man's relationship with others and himself
- Concepts about man's relationship with God's created world.

Need for Selection of Concepts

If you have done any teaching, you have already found that after spending many hours studying a Bible passage, you always have more to teach than you will have time to teach. A passage may have many concepts. One of the mistakes teachers make is to try to focus on too many of the concepts in a passage. Because they feel that all are so important, they try to focus on them all. So they splatter their students with many ideas, and the result often is confusion rather than clarity.

The fewer the concepts emphasized, the greater will be the learning. It is better that your students gain a clear insight into a few concepts rather than a fuzzy view of many. Here are some things to keep in mind when selecting concepts.

1. In your personal study, try to summarize the key ideas or concepts in a passage. Ask yourself: What are the key ideas in this passage?

2. Write these concepts in terms of the *now*, not just as an historical fact, but as a relevant teaching for today.

3. Write your concepts in sentence form, in words that have meaning to you.

4. Try to state only one concept in each sentence.

5. Of the many you might teach, select only those which you will have time to focus on.

6. In the selecting, try to focus on those concepts that are the heart of the passage. Avoid selecting the less important ones, even though they may be relevant ideas.

Remember that the sharper in focus you have the concepts, the more easily your students will grasp them. Often students are confused in a Bible study, because the teachers themselves really are not clear as to what they are trying to emphasize.

How to State Concepts

Let us imagine you are to conduct a Bible study on John 4, the story of the Samaritan woman's encounter with Jesus. This story can be divided into several sections: 4:1-6; 7-15; 18-26; 27-30; 39-42. In the study of this story, if you focused on the key words, you would discover that the action centers around three words: water, worship, and witness. These words also symbolize the three main aspects of the Christian relationships.

As you analyze the teachings in this story, you will discover many other concepts, but these three main ones can be stated thus:

- Water is the true symbol of all that Christ seeks to give us.
- Worship is our response to what Christ offers us.
- Witnessing is a natural outcome when Christ becomes meaningful to us.

After you have identified the main concepts, then you should try to formulate supporting ones relating to these main ideas. Here is an example of supporting concepts for the first one.

- Water is the true symbol of all that Christ seeks to give us.
  - Jesus Christ is able to quench the deepest thirst.
  - Jesus Christ gives eternal life to all who believe in him.

When you have stated your concepts so that they are sharp and clear in your own mind, you will find planning your session activities much easier. You know what you want your students to discover. If you have a very limited time for teaching the passage, you may have to limit your focus to one of the key concepts in the passage. If in the beginning of the study, you have your students identify the key words, they can be helped to discover the three main concepts in the passage. After they have gained an understanding of the whole story as summarized in the three words, then they will be satisfied if you focus on any of the aspects which you wish to select. Sometimes when teaching a Bible study, it is better to focus on one aspect which you study in depth, rather than skim over all the teachings.

Formulating the Objectives

Defining Objectives

Selecting the focus is a two-pronged process: deciding *what* you will focus on and *why*. Concepts have to do with the *what*. Objectives have to do with the *why*.

The dictionary defines the *objective* as an aim, an end of action, a point to be reached. Objectives have to do with goals, purposes, reasons for doing something, outcomes. When you plan a Bible study, you need to consider what you hope this Bible study will accomplish in the life of your learner. You might ask yourself this question: through this Bible study, what will my learners be able to do, feel or understand that they were not able to do or feel or understand before the session? Your concern should be with learner outcomes.

Concepts and *objectives* are very closely related. The *concept* expresses a key idea or attitude or skill which you hope to communicate to your learners. The *objective* expresses the way you would like your learner to respond to the concept: *understand* or *appreciate* or *recognize* or *identify*, etc. As a teacher you cannot always control the way a learner will respond, but you can plan for the ways you hope he will respond.

Formulating Objectives

While all teachers may have some kind of objectives in mind when they plan a Bible lesson, not all think that it is important to formulate their objectives in definite statements. Too often teachers have as their objective, "to cover the Bible passage." Formulating definite objectives will enable you to:

- determine how to plan your session activities
- evaluate the learning during the lesson
- evaluate the learning after the session.

There are two common ways to state objectives: in terms of the actions of the teacher and in terms of the outcomes in the life of the learner.

IN TERMS OF THE ACTIONS OF THE TEACHER

You might find objectives stated this way:

- To teach the story of the woman at the well
- To show how the story reveals the three aspects of the Christian life
- To help them apply the story to themselves.

As you study these objectives, you will note that the objectives are general, and the focus is on the teacher and what he is going to do during the class session. The objectives do not reflect a specific concept to be emphasized nor do they define what are to be the outcomes in the life of the learner. While you as the teacher might think you are doing some of these things, you have no criteria by which you can evaluate the learning that may be taking place.

IN TERMS OF LEARNER OUTCOMES

A better way to state objectives is in terms of learner outcomes relating to a concept. An objective should reflect the concept to which a learner is to respond. Study the following objectives. Note how they reflect the concepts on page 29.

Through the study of this story, it is intended that the participants will

- discover the three aspects of the Christian life as revealed in the story through the key words: water, worship, witness.
- identify ways in which each is a significant aspect.
- describe how the aspects have been operating in their own lives.

These objectives express learner outcomes. They may be general in nature, but they focus on the learner and his response. Note that each objective begins with a verb. Objectives can be expressed in terms of *knowledge* you would like the learners to gain, in terms of *attitudes* you hope they might develop, and in terms of *actions* which might grow out of the knowledge learned and attitudes developed.

The more specific are your objectives, the more easily you can measure the effectiveness of your session.

As you study these objectives, note their characteristics:

- They begin with a verb.
- They reflect a concept which is being emphasized.
- They are specific.
- They focus on learner activities and outcomes.

Problems

As I share with you these suggestions concerning concepts and objectives, I am well aware that I am focusing on that aspect of session planning which we as teachers most often neglect. In planning for a session, we are usually concerned about the interpretation of a passage and procedures for teaching it, but we don't force ourselves to define precisely our concepts and objectives.

One of the reasons is that identifying concepts and formulating objectives is difficult. We think we can teach a reasonably effective lesson without being so precise about our concepts and objectives.

But even though we do find the stating of concepts and objectives difficult, the struggle in the process has value. We need to force ourselves to think seriously about what teachings should be emphasized and what we hope might be learner outcomes. Otherwise we can be slipshod and superficial in our teaching.

As you work on your session plan, anticipate the process to be cyclical. After you have isolated what you consider some of the key ideas, write some tentative concepts and objectives. Then consider some possible procedures for accomplishing the objectives. As you work with the procedures, you may rewrite your concepts and objectives. Expect that you may have to go "round and round" as you plan a session. There are many ways to state concepts and formulate objectives, and you may revise yours several times before you feel satisfied.

CHAPTER 7

Planning Your Process

So far in our focus on teaching we have considered the *teacher, the learners, the concepts and objectives.* Now we shall consider the *process,* the means by which we are to accomplish our objectives.

Process has to do with organization, methods, strategy, materials, resources. As we think about the ideas which we want to emphasize in the Bible passage and the objectives which we hope to accomplish, we have to decide what methods and materials to use and how best to organize the lesson. There is no best way for communicating ideas and accomplishing objectives. The ideas and objectives themselves might give direction to the process, but there are many possibilities: lecture, visual and audio aids, discussion, exploration, skits, role play, panels, debates, drama, reports, interviews, questions, projects, creative expression. These are just a few of the many things you might do in your teaching session. Whatever you do, you need to work out a step-by-step plan of the experiences in which you want to involve your students.

Sometimes persons have asked, "Is it necessary to make a careful plan for a Bible study? Is it not enough just to pray and meditate on the passage? Then won't the Holy Spirit guide you in how to teach the passage in the class itself? Can't we limit the Holy Spirit with carefully devised plans?"

My answer is that indeed it is possible to conduct a Bible study without working out a definite plan of procedure, but it may not be very effective. There are few persons to whom the Lord has given such a rare gift that they can teach effectively without formulating a plan. The most effective Bible teachers I have witnessed have always given evidence of thorough study and careful planning. To be sure, when a person teaches the Bible, he is not alone in the process. He has the assurance that the Holy Spirit is working through the Word. But the influence of the Holy Spirit is more often limited than enhanced by casual planning.

Selecting the Process

If you have not done much teaching, you may be nervous about conducting the Bible study. You are apt to think that the entire burden of the success of this Bible study rests on your shoulders. You feel that your students will expect you to be the expert in knowledge. Possibly you would like to involve the learners in discovery methods, but are afraid they will not respond. It seems to you that the easiest and safest way is to lecture.

But conducting an effective lecture can be just as difficult as other kinds of teaching. When you learn how to involve persons in a variety of techniques, you will find there are many approaches to teaching. This does not mean that we might not lecture at times in our studies, but it means we use the lecture where it can be the most effective.

In the next chapter I shall describe a variety of methods you might use when seeking to involve your learners in the Bible study. But first let us consider some general things to remember when planning your session.

Build your session on process rather than person.

Possibly you wonder what is meant by this statement. To build a session on *process* means that you plan your session activities so carefully that they in themselves will carry the lesson. You as the teacher can function as the facilitator. Too often teachers plan their sessions rather loosely, hoping that they will be able to ask the right questions at the appropriate times. When they do this, they are building their session on a *person*, that person, being themselves.

Instead of carefully formulating the questions and activities they might use, they hope they will think up the questions and activities on the spur of the moment, as the need arises. They carry the burden of the session and too often they find it is a heavier burden than they bargained for. Few people are able to think up stimulating questions on the spur of the moment. The questions they ask are usually simple observation or the *yes* and *no* kind. The learners may not respond very readily to the questions, and the teacher ends up bombarding them with more questions or answering them himself.

It takes practice to learn how to build a session on *process* rather than on *yourself*, but in the end you will find your teaching easier and more satisfying. In Chapter 8 we suggest many things which you might do in building a session on process.

Know the purpose for each of your activities.

You should organize your session in a logical order, with each activity growing out of the previous one. You should also have clearly in mind the purpose for each of your activities, how each relates to the over-all objectives. It is very possible to have fascinating and stimulating activities which are ends in themselves. They do little for helping your learners gain insight in the Bible passage.

An activity may have any one of the following purposes:

- To introduce the theme of your study
- To stimulate interest in the study
- To guide learners to observe the facts
- To guide the learners to interpret
- To challenge the learners to personalize the Bible teachings in terms of their daily living
- To challenge their thinking, with no intention of the students coming to a conclusion
- To enable students to summarize and evaluate learnings.

Plan the timing of activities.

You not only plan your activities, but you also need to plan the amount of time you wish to spend on each one. Unless you do this, the temptation is to spend too much time on beginning activities and not have time for some of the later ones, which may be more important to your lesson. Being a timekeeper is one of the important roles of a teacher. You have to learn how to move your students along so that they do not get bogged down in non-essentials.

You can do this best if you plan the tentative amount of time to give to each activity. This does not mean that time becomes a tyrant, but a reminder. Plan your teaching to fit in your time allotment. Avoid having so much to cover that you must "fly" through the material.

Use as many senses as possible.

We learn through our senses: hearing, seeing, touching, smelling, tasting. We may not use all of these in a Bible study, but the more we use, the more potentials for learning. For this reason, even though you are lecturing, you should involve your learners in some type of visual aids: chalk boards, maps, flip charts, diagrams, pictures, etc. Since persons retain only about 10 percent of what they hear, unless you tie their hearing with some "sight," they will not remember much of what you say. Also it is very possible to use the senses of smelling, touching and tasting to enhance a study.

For example, have your learners munch on grapes as they consider the teachings in John 15 on bearing fruit. Have them drink water as they discuss Jesus' claim to be the living water in John 4. Have them eat bread as they consider his claim to be the Bread of Life.

CHAPTER 8

Enabling Persons to Discover

In this chapter are suggestions for helping persons observe, interpret, summarize, and personalize the teachings in a Bible study. Some of the suggestions can be used in an assignment, and some of them can be used during the class session. Naturally, you will never use them all with one study. They are lists from which you select those processes which will best accomplish your objectives.

Enabling Persons to Discover

1. Have them look for key words.

One of the easiest ways to begin observing a passage is to have your students look for key words. This is easy for them because there are no "right" or "wrong" words. Everything they select is OK. This will give even the timid student a sense of freedom and a willingness to try. You might have them underline the words in their Bible. In the very beginning of your study, encourage them to mark their Bible with colored pencils. If they are to read a long passage, such as a chapter, have them look for key words, section by section, or paragraph by paragraph. Do not spend very much time on this process. Do it rather quickly, knowing that you will return again to some of the sections.

After they have noted some of the key words in a section, have them share what they observed, and try to select what they think are *the* key words. Sometimes one or two words or phrases stand out very sharply, and it is not difficult to select what are the key ones. After they have determined what are some of the key ones, then have them try to summarize the key thought in each paragraph. Sometimes you can summarize the key thought with one of the key words.

As we have already stated in Chapter 6, the John 4 account of the Samaritan woman at the well is an example of a story that can be summarized in three key words: water, worship, witness. By having your students read each paragraph and look for key words, they can discover for themselves these three key ideas.

2. Have them look for other specific details.

Usually a Scripture passage has certain literary characteristics. Since you have made a thorough study of the passage, you will know what they are and can guide your learners to look for them. Here are some suggestions:

a. If the passage is strong in comparisons or contrasts, have them look for these. They might divide a sheet of paper, listing the comparison or contrasts, or you might do this on the chalkboard or chart.

b. If there are many admonitions, have them look for these, underlining them in their Bibles, or recording them in some way. You might have them look for the imperative verbs—those that tell them to do something.

c. If a passage has a list of items, have them study the list and consider what is the relationship of the items to each other. Have them analyze the list for progression in thought.

d. If there are many repetitions, significant connectives, etc., have them look for these things.

e. If your passage is narrative, use the words *who, when, where, what, how, why,* as guide words for noting details in the story.

Try to suggest a procedure which will most quickly give them insight into the details of the passage. Have them look for those details which are most noticeable in the passage and will best help them observe its content. Beware of "dragging" your learners through a passage verse by verse with such observation questions as: "What do you see in this verse?" They may see nothing! And become very bored!

3. Use a structural diagram of passage.

Another effective way for helping persons observe the details in a passage is to provide them with a structural diagram of the Bible passage. To do this, you type the passage in the center of a page, separating the units of thought in as graphic a way as possible so that the passage can be more easily analyzed, somewhat like the psalms are printed in the Bible. If you wonder what I mean by a "structural diagram," note the examples on pages 21, 30, and Chapter 8 in *The Joy of Discovery in Bible Study.*

Then in your class session, have your learners make their observations directly on the structural diagram. Of course this means that you will need to provide copies of the structural diagram. This is a helpful approach for beginning teachers who may have difficulty stimulating discussions. Let me tell you about one such teacher.

Mary was a nurse. She had strong feelings against teaching because her few attempts had been very frustrating and defeating. But her church talked her into conducting one of the adult Bible classes. One day she came to me, very discouraged. "I don't know what to do with the class or the material. It does not seem to help us, and the group is not very responsive. I can't get much discussion going."

I looked at the study guide she was using, one on the book of Amos, and noted that the questions focused on small sections and were more or less simple observation ones. I could see immediately that the guide itself was not very challenging or stimulating.

So I took the Bible and studied the chapter itself to see what it contained. The next lesson was to focus on sections of Amos 4. As I read Amos 4 aloud, I became enthralled by the very way the chapter was written, noting the ever recurring phrase: " 'Yet you did not return to me,' says the Lord."

"Oh, Mary," I said, "you must not study this magnificent chapter piecemeal! The dynamics of the message is in the very structure of the passage. Note how each section of verses describes the judgments which the Lord brought to the people, hoping they would turn from their wicked ways. Note the recurring statement, 'Yet you did not return to me.' "

I suggested that she make a structural diagram of the passage, showing her how to do it. Then I showed her how to have her students analyze the entire chapter by looking for key words in each section, summarizing the key thought in each section, underlining some of the key connectives and the recurring statement. I suggested a few general thought questions to consider after they had observed the passage.

The next week when I saw Mary I did not have to ask her how the class went. The broad grin on her face told me all I needed to know. "Our class was just wonderful," she exclaimed. "I brought them each a copy of the passage. We analyzed it as you said. We saw so many things to discuss, we never finished. And do you know what one asked me, 'Are you a professional teacher?' Me, who never wanted to teach!"

Analyzing a structural diagram of the passage made the difference.

Enabling Persons to Interpret

While you can have your students observe the entire passage, you cannot have them interpret everything. Usually your time is too short in any class session to focus on the meaning of everything. Thus you have to be selective in what to interpret, selecting those things which are most crucial for understanding the message in the passage. Here are some things you might do.

1. Divide the sections of a passage among the students.

Don't have them all try to interpret everything. Divide the passage among the students, several on each section or set of verses. Or you might have them just focus on some of the key words, but even so you divide the words among the students, so each group of students focuses on only a few key ideas. Thus you divide responsibilities. You need to allow time for them to discuss the meanings among themselves and then share with the entire group.

2. Invite questions.

Sometimes it is helpful to invite your students to identify those areas which they do not understand. Encourage them to ask questions about statements in a passage. Sometimes, you might give each student or small group of students a verse or two and have them ask a question about the key thoughts in the verse. This way you try to teach them how to ask questions. At first persons do not even know how to ask questions for understanding. You can help them by having them use the following kinds of questions:

What is the meaning of . . . ?　　What is the implication of . . . ?

What is the significance of . . . ?　　What is the relationship with . . . ?

3. Use a variety of devices for interpreting.

Have your students do some of the things you have done for interpreting a passage. To do some of these things, you will have to provide the extra books and materials.

a. Have them compare translations. This will always give new insights into a passage.

b. Have them study cross-references. You might have to provide these because they may not know where to find them. If you are using several references, have them written on cards to give to students.

c. Have them define words. Provide a dictionary for them to look up definitions. If you have no dictionary, have them try to define terms in their own words, from their own experiences.

4. Wrestle with meanings.

Even after students have done some of the above things, they still need to be challenged to wrestle with meanings, using what they gained in their study and their own knowledge and background.

5. Compare analogies.

If your learners are trying to analyze the meaning of a key word in terms of the Christian life, first have them think of the actual meaning or characteristics of the word. Then have them make the analogy to the spiritual life. For instance, in the story of the Samaritan woman, Jesus speaks of being the "water of life." First have your learners analyze the characteristics of water and its value for physical life. Then have them apply these facts to the spiritual life.

6. Use reaction statements.

One way to have learners discuss meanings is to provide a series of statements to which they are to react: *agree* or *disagree*.

7. Use open-ended statements.

Another way is to give them open-ended statements to complete. For instance, "I think to worship God in Spirit means . . . ."

8. Present several views.

Present several interpretations of a passage and have the students debate about the interpretations.

9. Paraphrase a passage.

Have the students try to paraphrase some parts of a passage in their own words.

10. Use magazine and newspaper clippings.

Provide newspaper or magazine clippings, pictures, articles, cartoons, advertisements, headlines for use in discussing the meanings of key ideas.

Enabling Persons to Personalize Bible Teachings
Importance

While it is important to help persons *observe* and *interpret* the teachings in a passage, it is equally important to provide opportunities for them to *personalize* the teachings. In fact, this aspect of Bible study interests people most. One common complaint is, "We spend so much time observing and interpreting that we never have time to relate the teachings to our lives."

This is a valid criticism which we as teachers need to take seriously. It is through the sharing of personal reactions that persons most often become "ministers" to each other and learn how to become "ministers" to those in their outside world. Personalization offers opportunities for these important aspects of Bible study:

- time to verbalize their feelings
- time to realize their own creative potentials
- time to learn to know each other better
- time to discover others have similar problems
- time to affirm and encourage each other
- time to take off masks and be honest with each other
- time to be blessed as they hear how the Lord has worked in others' lives.

Possibilities

There are countless ways persons might share their insights and feelings regarding Bible teachings. We shall consider them in four areas.

VERBAL—expressing ideas through words
- Paraphrase passages
- Write poems, prayers, meditations
- Write letter expressing insights and feelings to a friend
- Complete open-ended statements such as: "My idea of grace is . . ."
- Complete open-ended short stories
- Provide multiple choices reflecting ways to respond
- Make an acrostic with some word such as *faith* or *prayer,* etc.
- Share personal experiences
- Identify with the problems of Bible characters.

VISUAL—expressing ideas through visual senses
- Make a montage, collage using magazine pictures and objects
- Make a banner, poster, slogan, chart
- Make a rebus—a riddle using pictures and symbols
- Illustrate using crayons, paint, felt pens, etc.
- Depict a concept using paper, wire, tinfoil, yarn, and other materials
- Use clippings from newspaper, articles, pictures, cartoons, headlines, advertisements for stimulating discussions
- Select objects which are symbolic of some Christian truth.

MUSIC—expressing ideas through songs and music
- Write a song to some familiar hymn
- Write a song and tune to a Scripture passage
    - first stanza contains words of Scripture
    - second stanza contains meaning of verse
    - third stanza reflects how to relate verse in life
- Select a hymn which reflects the message of a Scripture passage
- Listen to music and express feelings which it invokes.

DRAMA—expressing ideas through actions
- Write choral readings from Scripture
- Role-play some of the ideas in Scripture
- Dramatize some of the narratives
- Pantomime the message in a passage
- Write dramatic readings.

Remember that it is not the end-product but the process that has value. Most persons feel that they have no creative talents. When you suggest that they express their feelings or insights in some of these ways, their first reaction is usually negative. Remind them that all persons have potentials for creativity. To create is to produce something that is their own. Each person has within himself ideas that if expressed will be a blessing to the rest of a group. Remind them that this is not an art or music project, but a sharing of ideas. Whatever one does can be a blessing to the others.

CHAPTER 9

Relating to the Learner

The normal title for this chapter might be "Presenting the Bible Study." As we stated in Chapter 3, there are three general areas which a teacher must consider when conducting a Bible study: 1) your personal study; 2) your preparation of a session plan; 3) your involvement in the teaching session. In this chapter we are focusing on the third area.

I do not want to use the phrase *presenting the lesson* because that suggests the picture of the teacher standing before his students "giving them something." I wanted to use a title which suggests the role of the teacher as a part of the learning experience. Even though you come to the Bible study with a basket full of biblical "goodies," I would like you always to view yourself as one coming also to learn, rather than coming to present all of your "goodies." Remember that your students may have some "goodies" also which you can enjoy.

The tendency of many teachers is to view their session in terms of *teaching* rather than learning. One time a teacher asked me how many psalms I thought he could teach during a series of ten Sunday morning sessions. I said, "If you are interested only in teaching, present as many as you want to. If you are interested in learning, I doubt that you can involve your students in more than a couple each time if you want to go into an in-depth study."

When teachers express frustration about "covering the lesson" and "getting things across," I know that their focus is more on teaching than on learning. We all get caught in the trap of having lots of wonderful insights to share with our students and feeling frustrated that we can't "give" them all that we have to give. If our concern is mainly teaching content, then our tendency is to "pour it on," covering as much as we can in our time allotment. While lots of "teaching" might be going on, there is a serious question as to how much learning is taking place.

If we are concerned about learning, then we need to analyze our teaching session from the learner's point of view: What are the best

ways persons learn? How much can my learners grasp in the time allotment? What are the most effective ways to stimulate learning?

Clues to Effective Teaching

Every teacher wants to be an effective teacher, to feel that his students are learning. But what is effective teaching? For many years effective teaching was measured by the amount of *knowledge* a person
gained but educators began to realize that learning is more than gaining knowledge. Learning also has to do with *attitudes* and *actions*. It
is emotionalizing and actualizing the knowledge. Some educators con-
tend that no one has truly learned something until he has *internalized*
the truths to which he has been exposed, until he *actualizes* them in
his life. Thus we see that effective Bible teaching is more than enabling persons to grasp biblical truths. The teaching must be of such a
nature that our learners will respond positively to the teachings and
integrate them in their lives.

Let us recall again Barclay's statement: *"It is only when truth is
discovered that it is appropriated. When a man is simply told the
truth, it remains external to him and he can quite easily forget it.
When he is led to discover the truth himself it becomes an integral
part of him and he never forgets."* If we accept this statement as valid,
then we might say that *an effective teacher is one who enables learners
to discover truths and actualize them in their lives.*

As a conscientious teacher, you might still ask the question: How
can I know if I am an effective teacher? Are there any clues? The purpose of this chapter is to provide some of those clues which make for
effective teaching.

The material in this chapter reflects the insights I have gained about
the teaching-learning process through observing countless practice-
teaching sessions. During the last ten years, I have been involved in
helping persons learn how to teach the Bible more effectively. In
micro-teaching sessions from five to fifteen minutes in length, students
practiced on each other, teaching a small section in the Bible. Sometimes they worked as teams and sometimes individually. They would
have a class from six to eight in number.

Always there were some "observers" who critiqued the sessions. The
observers were to record all of the evidences of effective teaching which
they observed. The emphasis was not on what was "good or bad" or
"right or wrong" but what were the most effective approaches. The
contention was that all teachers had a measure of effectiveness. The
purpose of these micro-teaching sessions was to affirm the teacher in
his effectiveness and to help him develop greater effectiveness.

The effectiveness of a teaching session is dependent on many things:
personal relationships, organization, use of materials, physical environ-
ment, kinds of learning activities, student involvement in the learning

activities. As persons observed the micro-sessions, they were to focus on many of these aspects of teaching. Through the observations, many clues to effective teaching evolved. Some of these aspects have been discussed in previous chapters.

In this and the next chapter we shall focus on other aspects that are crucial in determining the effectiveness of teaching. First we shall consider ways to develop satisfying personal relationships.

Developing Personal Relationships

When inexperienced teachers seek help in learning how to teach, the questions they most often ask are: What do I do? How do I do it? Teachers accept the fact that to teach they must *do* something. But before teachers consider what they must *do*, they should always consider first what they must *be* to their students. The *being* often determines the effectiveness of the *doing*.

The way a student feels about us as teachers greatly influences how he will respond to our teaching. We can have all kinds of students in our classes but all have the same inner yearnings to be liked and to be accepted. Their satisfaction in a class is increased as they are made to feel they "belong" and have value. Students are very sensitive to a teacher's attitudes and actions. There are many things which we can do to develop positive relationships with our learners.

1. Establish an informal setting.

Unless you have a very large group, try to arrange as informal a setting as possible. Have your students sit around tables or in a circle so that they may see each other's faces. If your group is large, sometimes it is possible to arrange the chairs in several semicircles so that they still can see some of the group. If I am to conduct a Bible study and find all of the chairs in straight rows, if they are movable, I will take the time to rearrange the chairs before I begin the lesson. As soon as the chairs are rearranged so that persons can see each other, the atmosphere changes. People become more relaxed and willing to share. When I am asked how to get persons to discuss in a Bible study, I say that the first criteria is an informal setting in which they can see each other. If possible, I will sit with the group, rather than stand. This increases the feeling of relaxed informality.

2. Be friendly and concerned.

The way we greet persons, use their names, and show interest in their personal lives are important factors in establishing positive relationships. If we as teachers reveal interest in these areas, our students will feel that we are concerned about them as persons, rather than just as objects to "save" or "indoctrinate" or "convert."

43

3. Be accepting and affirming to responses.

Use every opportunity in a class to make each person feel that what he or she has to say is important to you. There are three levels of communication: 1) the *verbal*, those words which we use in speaking; 2) the *non-verbal*, those body actions, postures and motions used when speaking; 3) the *extra-verbal*, those feelings and attitudes reflected between words and actions. We consciously or unconsciously reflect our acceptance or rejection of persons through our facial expressions, tone of voice, and body actions, aside from our words.

We can reinforce the efforts and contributions of students in verbal ways by using such comments as "Thanks for sharing"; "interesting"; "thoughtful"; "good idea"; "I hadn't thought of that before." Thus we give some kind of response which says to the student that we heard what he said and respected his view. We can also affirm them in non-verbal ways by nodding the head, smiling, eye contact, or gesture of our hands.

4. Be open to differing views.

In a Bible class there is the possibility of differing views or interpretations. It is important that you encourage differing views so that all sides can be heard. Try to show respect for the differing views even though you may not agree with some of them. After you have encouraged all to share their views, then students appreciate the teacher sharing his view. But try to avoid putting anyone down just because he states a view other than yours.

5. Avoid embarrassing students.

Without realizing what we are doing, we can sometimes embarrass and discourage those in a class by our responses to some of their answers. If we cut down their answers, ignore them, or say their answer is incorrect, our students will begin to hesitate sharing. If a student gives an incorrect answer or one that we feel is too "far out," one way is to invite the others to share their interpretations. Often the other students will give interpretations which will offset the incorrect or "far-out" one.

If a person is having difficulty answering a question, we can try rewording the question or give an illustration. Sometimes pointing directly to a verse in the passage will help. Or affirm them in their struggle with such statements as: "Thanks for your willingness to share"; "I appreciate your difficulty to state your feelings or thoughts"; "This is not an easy passage to interpret." Do everything in your power to help students feel you are sensitive to their struggles in sharing.

When asking questions, it is best to call for volunteers rather than to call on individuals, unless you know the person will not be embarrassed.

6. Encourage relationships between students.

Encourage students to work with each other, be enablers to each other, be open and considerate of each other. That is the reason it is important to provide ways in which students can work with each other, involving them in "team learning." As they work together in a group—sharing, challenging, questioning—they can be of great help to each other, learn from each other, encourage and affirm each other, help each other identify gifts and strengths.

The Bible class should be more than a time for gathering information. The atmosphere in the Bible class should be such that persons become free to share their problems and concerns and invite the rest of them to pray with them about the problems. It should incorporate the true meaning of *koinonia,* a fellowship of believers where persons come together with a genuine sharing of the things that are theirs in Christ, a real caring for one another, and a real baring of their souls to one another. If a small-group Bible study cannot provide this kind of fellowship, where can persons find it?

7. Be open and honest with students.

Don't come as the expert, but as a learner, not only in terms of information about the Bible, but also in terms of your own personal needs. Take off your mask and share with your students your doubts and concerns, your feelings, your hopes and joys. Try to identify with their problems, and they will also quickly identify with yours. They can more quickly identify with your problems than they can identify with your successes.

CHAPTER 10

Increasing the Potentials for Learning

While your personal relationship with your students is very important, the manner in which you involve them in the learning activities is equally important. They want to be liked, but they also want to learn something. Even though you have a well-developed session plan, its effectiveness does depend on the way you execute it. In this chapter we shall focus on some facets in teaching which have the potential for increasing the effectiveness of a session.

1. Prepare students carefully for each activity.

It is very important that your students be prepared carefully for each activity. Students become confused if they do not know what they are to do or why. Here are some things to do:

- Reflect your theme and key concepts in your opening remarks. State very clearly what you intend to emphasize in the Bible study.

- Give specific things to look for whenever you ask persons to read a Bible passage. Example: "As you read this passage, note the imperatives and contrasts."

- Give directions one at a time when you are explaining something for them to do.

- Define words and give background information if they are needed to understand the passage they are to study.

2. Make smooth bridges between activities.

Learners become very frustrated if they do not see purpose in what they are doing. They want to know *why* and *how* each activity relates to the ojectives of the lesson, to the whole session. Therefore, it is very important that you make smooth transitions between activities, summarizing what has been discussed and explaining what is the next activity. If in the previous activity you have listed items on the board, then you might read these again in your summarizing statement.

The bridge has value because it is the way in which you can tie together all of your activities and show purpose for each one. It is also the way in which you can continually emphasize your key concepts. One additional advantage is that through the bridge you can bring your students back to the main focus if they get sidetracked in a discussion.

3. Allow students to do their own thinking.

One of the temptations of a Bible teacher is to do the thinking for the students. We have them read a passage and then proceed to tell them what is in the passage. For some reason we seem to think that our telling is more effective than their discovering. While a few students may want their teacher to do their thinking, many become frustrated. Try to devise methods so that your students can do as much of their own thinking as possible. In Chapter 7-8 on process, there are many suggestions as to ways you can challenge your students to do their own thinking.

4. Have your students use their Bibles.

This might seem to be a strange admonition. Surely if a person is conducting a Bible study, he will have his students use their Bibles. Yet this admonition is directed at two problems which are sometimes present at Bible studies. Persons do not always have Bibles with them and the teachers do not always use them even if they do. The temptation not to use the Bible is especially great if we as teachers are lecturing. We can become so involved in what we are "giving" to our students that we forget to focus their attention on the passage we are explaining. And if we are running out of time, we can be tempted to rush through our lecture and skip all reading of Bible verses.

As far as learning is concerned, unless you direct the attention of your students to the verses you are explaining, they may not remember much of what you say. They may be inspired but they are more apt to take with them the "words of the teacher" than the "words of the Bible."

The Use of the Chalkboard

The chalkboard can be one of the best aids a Bible teacher has. If properly used, it will easily double the effectiveness of a lesson. For the chalkboard to be an effective teaching device, there are several things to keep in mind.

1. Aim to have the board work progressive.

It should be placed on the board as the lesson proceeds. To have a chart on the board before the period begins may save time for the teacher, but it does not aid in the process of learning. The teacher sets up competition for himself. The class will be so busy reading and copying what is on the board that the members will not hear what the teacher is saying. If you want a chart on the board, then quickly go through it before you focus on any one aspect.

2. Aim to have the board work purposeful.

The class should sense the purpose and aim of the lesson through the board work. Thus, as the lesson progresses, the students should see the whole message unfold before their eyes.

3. Try to use the suggestions of the group.

Aim to catch the meaning of a person's suggestion, even though you write a different word.

4. Try to show relationships.

Draw arrows, underline words, place a question mark near a comment. Use lines, brackets, summary words.

5. Aim to have your board work useful.

One of the main values of having a chart or diagram on the board is that it can be used as the basis for both interpretation and application. When the students have in front of them a summary of the Bible passage, they can more easily analyze, interpret, and apply. A chart is also helpful if the class time is limited. The teacher can give a bird's-eye view of the whole and have the group discuss just those parts for which there is time.

6. Try to have your board work helpful.

It is possible for board work to be a hindrance to teaching. Some of the following practices can become distracting to the lesson:

- Writing aimlessly all over the board
- Writing too much so that the class becomes bored
- Writing too small or illegibly
- Writing too slowly
- Writing, erasing and rewriting too many times.

7. Remember your role as the leader.

View yourself as the "midwife" helping the group give birth to its own thoughts, ideas, or solutions. Your role is often that of a recorder, interpreter, questioner, and summarizer.

Use of Flip Charts and Study Sheets

A flip chart is a very useful aid in teaching and has some advantages over the chalkboard. It is movable and can be used in all kinds of situations. You can prepare the charts before your session and can use them as they fit in with your teaching plan. Here are some things to place on the chart:

- questions to use in your session
- statements for reaction
- diagrams, graphs, and charts
- Bible verses and songs.

Study sheets also have value in a teaching session but you have to have some way to duplicate them. The study sheet can serve as a "track" for your session. It should be simple and progressive. Beware of having too many questions or statements on it. Students can become bored if they spend the session writing answers on a study sheet. One of its greatest values is its use for home study. A study sheet might contain some of these things:

- structural diagram of the passage
- observation and interpretive questions
- open-ended statements
- reaction statements
- quotations
- ways to respond.

The Use of Questions
Purpose of Asking Questions

Many teachers have a misunderstanding as to the purpose of asking questions. They think of questions only as a means for testing a student's knowledge. If the pupil has enough memorized knowledge to answer the questions, the teacher feels that the lesson has been well taught. If the student cannot answer the questions, the teacher is apt to feel that his teaching has been a failure.

The "testing" question has its place in the teaching program, but a question can be much more than a *probe* to find what the student knows. It can be the sharp *instrument* which cuts into the darkness and lets in the light of understanding. It can be the means to help students think and make good decisions. It can be the key to help them open doors to new insights and knowledge. When you as a teacher ask questions, you must be conscious of your purpose. You must consider what you want to accomplish through your questions.

Kinds of Questions to Ask

Questions may be classified in many ways. We shall use terms which are especially applicable to Bible study:

1. *Observation and factual questions:* to help the members of your group note the significant facts in a passage.

2. *Explanatory and relationship questions:* to help them analyze the meaning and relationships of the facts.

3. *Search and thought questions:* to help them consider the implication and significance of the facts.

4. *Application and correlation questions:* to help them apply the truths to their own lives and to correlate them with other biblical truths.

Effects Questions Have on the Learner

Whereas the teacher may think of questions as factual or thought-provoking, the student will analyze them in a different way. He will think of them in relation to his emotional and mental reaction. To him a question may be "telling," "trying," "testing" or "teaching."

1. *The "telling" question:* This type is no challenge to the student. The question is so worded that he can guess at the answer without thinking. For example: "James says we should be careful with our tongues, doesn't he?" To such a question, students would merely nod their heads and go on dreaming. Questions which can be answered with just a "yes" or "no" border on the "telling" type.

2. *The "trying" question:* This type of question is stated in such a vague or general manner that the learner does not know how to answer it. The question may cause confusion in his mind or may create an attitude of indifference, a sense of "What is the use of trying to answer it?"

3. *The "testing" question:* This type seeks to find what knowledge the learner is gaining or has already acquired. Testing questions can be "trying" if the teacher is searching for knowledge that the learner has not yet acquired.

4. *The "teaching" question:* This type helps the learner take the facts which he has learned and use them in a concrete way in order to acquire new insights and concepts of truths. Also, it can help him gain new facts. To "teach" with your question means to guide, direct, and challenge your student in his thinking process.

EXAMPLES: Consider the kinds of questions you might ask relating to the story of Jesus on the cross in Luke 23:34-49:

Telling questions: The people at the cross called Jesus by many names, didn't they?

Testing questions: What titles did the various persons at the cross give

Jesus? What pronouns did the soldiers and the rulers use in referring to Jesus?

Teaching questions: What is the significance of the titles that the different persons gave to Jesus? What is the significance of the pronouns the soldiers and the rulers used relating to Jesus?

Clues to Asking Questions

1. Remember the purpose of the question in Bible study.

The question in the Bible class aims to *increase* the knowledge of your student. You want to help him *observe, think, gain insight* into biblical truths which he may not otherwise be able to do by himself. Through the question you will seek to cultivate his judgment and to increase his powers of observation and analyzation.

2. Construct your questions so that they are simple and specific, yet thought-provoking.

You want your students to find satisfaction in being able to discuss the questions, yet you want them to be challenged to think as they answer. Questions which are too easy bore people; those which are too difficult discourage them.

3. Write out your questions before your teaching session.

Plan your key ones and the order. Even though you may not use them in their original order or form, they will serve as your guide and give direction to your lesson.

4. Answer the questions which you have prepared.

Try to anticipate how your questions will affect your group and what various answers could be given. Revise and reconstruct the wording so as to make the question as clear and definite as possible.

5. Avoid "bombardment" of questions.

If we have not carefully thought through our questions before we teach, we tend to bombard our students with questions. Our first question may be very general or indefinite. We get no response so we begin to bombard our students with more and more questions. Usually the more we bombard them with questions, the less response we get. Often we end up having to answer our own questions.

6. Strive to use as few questions as possible, but have them well-planned.

For some Scripture passages, two or three questions might serve for the entire study. This is especially true in the study of narratives. As an example, the following questions could be used to help your students observe the details in the story of Jesus on the cross as recorded in Luke 23:32-49:

- Who are the persons in the story?
- What does each do?
- How does each respond to Jesus?
- How does he respond to them?

7. Allow time to consider questions.

It is difficult for most persons to answer questions off the "top of their heads." They can do better if given a few minutes to think about answers. Therefore, try to devise ways in which they do have some time to ponder on their answer. Here are some things you might do:

- Write your questions on cards and give each student one card.
- Write your questions on a large chart. This is especially helpful if you are using just a few questions for the entire study. Remember that students can respond more easily to a question they *see* than to one they *hear*.

8. Analyze the reaction of your group as you ask questions.

Study their response. Did they seem puzzled? Were they slow in responding? Did you receive the answers you expected? Which questions stimulated the most interest? Make note of these and study them for their characteristics.

9. Aim to be informal and spontaneous in your questions.

Seek to convey to your group that your purpose is to help them to discover *with you* the truths in the Bible passage. Give them the feeling that this study is a cooperative effort. You are not to pose as a teacher quizzing students, but to be a guide leading them in a search for truths. Keep the atmosphere relaxed and friendly.

The Joy of Discovery in Bible Study

As you have already discovered, Part One focuses on some of the general aspects of teaching Discovery Bible Study. Part Two contains specific instructions in how to help persons develop the basic skills in learning how to become discoverers. This skill course can be known as "The Joy of Discovery in Bible Study." The course might also be called "Discovery Skills in Bible Study" or "Methods in Bible Study."

The textbook for the course is *The Joy of Discovery in Bible Study*. The book provides the basis for all the activities in which persons will be involved in learning how to study their Bibles. Step-by-step instructions are provided for each learning experience.

Do not try to teach this course unless you have first been involved in the methods outlined in *The Joy of Discovery in Bible Study*. Your purpose for teaching the course must be built on the benefits which you have received in using these skills in your own personal Bible study and on your conviction that they have value for all persons. To be an effective teacher of this course, you have to have experience and be sold on the process.

CHAPTER 11

Introducing The Joy of Discovery in Bible Study

If you are studying this section of the book, I am assuming that you are interested in involving persons in the course, "The Joy of Discovery in Bible Study." It is important that you understand how this course differs in focus and purpose from other kinds of Bible studies. Here is a comparison:

Discovery Bible Study	Joy of Discovery in Bible Study
The focus is on the teachings in the Bible passage.	The focus is on developing skills to discover teachings.
The Bible passage is central in the teaching.	The Bible is used to develop the skills.
The purpose is to gain insight in the teachings.	The purpose is to develop skills to gain insight in Bible teachings.

General Purpose of the Course

Through the experiences designed in this course, it is intended that the participants will

1. Develop the skills which will increase their ability to *observe, interpret, summarize, evaluate, apply,* and *actualize* Bible teachings.

2. Discover the value of working together in learning teams.

3. Realize that the Bible has something to say to them personally.

4. Gain insight into their own potentials as students of the Bible.

Most congregations have Bible classes. The vast majority of these classes focus on a book or on some Bible topic. The primary purpose of most of the classes is to enable the students to gain insight into the teaching of some book or topic. While persons might learn some methods in Bible study, this is not the primary purpose of the studies.

Most people do not know how to study the Bible on their own. They are dependent on a teacher or some Bible course for direction. When they read the Bible individually, they usually focus mainly on how to apply it to their own lives. Many are honest enough to admit they really do not know what to do when left to their own devices, saying they get very little out of their Bibles when studying on their own.

One of the reasons we have congregations of people who do not know how to study on their own is that they have not been taught to do so. While leaders in congregations have promoted Bible study, there has not been this emphasis on helping persons become "discoverers." In fact, the opposite has been true. Too often Bible leaders have done the thinking for the people, causing people to develop a mental attitude: "I cannot do much studying on my own; the Bible is too difficult for me."

One of the first reactions persons have when they become involved in the skills of this course is that "they have to begin to think." Most of them have been so used to being spoon-fed that at first they become frustrated. They don't know how to *think,* and at first aren't sure if they even want to learn to *think!* But once they realize they have the capacity to think when they are studying, many become very enthusiastic about the process. As they say, they feel their fetters are broken and they become free persons.

It is important that you understand *what* you are doing and *why* if you plan to teach this course on skills in Bible study. In order to help you understand the rationale of the course, I shall share with you what I call the Big Ideas of the course. I suggest that you read them now, but they will not have much meaning to you until you begin to conduct the course. Then I suggest that you read them many times during the process. They need to become a part of the very fabric of your being.

The Big Ideas

Skills

You are always to keep in mind that you are teaching *skills* in Bible study. This is not a course on gaining deep insights into Bible passages, although this will also happen. It takes time to practice and develop skills, and not much Bible material can be covered.

Many times you will not be able to focus on all the teachings in a passage. Many times your heart will break when you have to skip a lot of the "goodies" in a passage because you do not have the time to discuss them. You will feel that it is almost sacrilegious to leave so many important passages sort of dangling in the air and not try to interpret them all. But this you must do when you are teaching skills. Some other time you can come back to the passage and focus on its content in more depth.

Enabler

This word describes the role of both the teacher and the participant. As leader you are to view your primary role as that of an *enabler*—you are to enable your participants to become "discoverers," to learn the skills required in becoming a "discoverer." You must see yourself on the sidelines coaching, stimulating, encouraging, facilitating, but they are to do the discovering.

Often you will feel tempted to preach little sermons on your favorite passages, but this you are not to do—your students are the ones to preach the sermons!

They, too, are to view themselves as enablers to each other. They are to enable each other to become discoverers by studying, sharing, affirming, challenging, encouraging each other.

Discovery

This idea has already been underscored several times. This term reflects the purpose of the course—to help persons become discoverers. As we have already said, the pattern for traditional Bible studies has been for the teacher to share his discoveries and for the student to be the listener. But in this course the role is changed. The student is to become the discoverer and is the first to share his insights. As the leader, you will add to their discoveries, but you are the last in the process—and only to enrich.

Involvement

This idea goes along with discovery. A person cannot become a discoverer without involvement. Persons must do their own observing, interpreting, summarizing, applying, and actualizing. Indeed, the students will vary with the amount of efforts they put into the study, some more than others. What a student gets out of the course will depend a great deal on the amount of involvement he invests in the process.

Team Learning

The participants are to work together as learning teams. They are to teach each other. (Read Chapter 14 in *The Joy of Discovery*.) Each participant is to do some individual study. Then in teams they share their discoveries, enriching each other's discoveries. No one is capable of observing or interpreting everything in a passage, but by individual study and sharing, they add to each other's knowledge—and to the leader's as well. Those who have been involved in this study agree that one of the biggest blessings in the course is how much they learn from each other.

Satisfaction

This is a very important aspect of this course. The learning of skills is not easy, and there will be a certain amount of frustration. The course is designed to introduce the skills very gradually so that the participants can have a measure of satisfaction all along the way. I have found that if persons are introduced to too many skills at one time or spend too little time on each skill, they become frustrated and discouraged. They are apt to think the process is too difficult for them and so reject the validity of the skills.

Some veteran Bible teachers may feel that the course does not lead persons deep enough into the Bible, that the process moves too slowly. Through 20 years of experience, I have found that if you try to go too fast, you can easily lose your students. When they learn the basic skills and find satisfaction in the doing, they can go as deep as they desire.

When persons first begin the study, they are so oriented to "right" or "wrong" ways to study Scripture that they keep wondering if what they do is "right" or "wrong." It takes much practice and encouragement for them to realize that they are not looking for "right" or "wrong" answers but that they are developing skills to increase their ability to discern what the Bible is saying to them.

Since they are not used to analyzing biblical teachings on their own, at first it is "scary." They need much encouragement from the leader so that they can gain confidence in their own ability to discover truths in the Bible.

Flexible

This word describes another attitude necessary for a leader to have. A person who is rigid in his opinions and approaches to the Bible may have difficulty teaching the course. You are to focus your concern on persons and what is happening to them, rather than on doctrines or interpretations.

In the beginning you need to be careful not to be critical of the contributions of your students. At first they may share rather shallow observations and even strange interpretations. They may not always be on the main point of what the passage really teaches. But you are to encourage them in their efforts. If you judge them for what they say, they may quickly become discouraged, concluding that they cannot become discoverers. Or they will just try to please you and try to say those things which they think you want them to say. They will lose the sense of freedom which you are trying to give them.

This is especially true in the realm of interpretation. They can come up with some rather strange interpretations, some which you may disagree with. But in the beginning, you need to be very cautious so that you do not discourage them in their efforts. You can always encourage other persons to share their interpretations—which may offset the view you consider strange. Try to help your students realize there are often several ways to interpret something. After the students have shared, then the leader can always add his view, but beware of condemning the others.

There are those who say, "Isn't it risky to teach persons how to become discoverers and learn how to interpret? Won't they go off on tangents? Shouldn't they be guided so that they will have the 'right' interpretation?" There are persons who feel that only the Bible scholars should study and teach the Bible, that it is too difficult a book for the "common" person. They feel that persons should always be guided so that they will come to know the "correct" interpretation of passages. This can be the view of both the liberal and the conservative.

To teach this course you have to believe in the integrity of the Bible and in the integrity of persons, that the Bible will reveal its message to all who come to it with an open mind and heart, and that all persons have the ability to gain insight into its teachings. The Bible is for the common person and in a measure can be understood by all. As for interpretations, even the scholars disagree on some interpretations, so will it be so serious for the lay persons in the church to vary in theirs? Actually, they need to learn how to discern and select the interpretations which they feel are the most true to the biblical account.

Organizing the Course

Your Learners

In teaching this course, your class should not be very large. Twelve is a good size for the class. This number provides flexibility with the members. They can work as teams of two, three, or four. Your learners can be older high-school students on through the retirement age. They can even be mixed in the same class and find fellowship and inspiration from each other. As the course is designed, I do not recommend it for junior-high persons, but many of the skills can be taught to them if introduced very gradually.

This is not a course for persons who have never studied their Bibles, that is, the very new Christian. This person needs a more elementary approach to the Bible.

This is specifically a course for persons who have done some Bible study, and long to get deeper into the Word, and to learn how to study on their own.

When inviting persons to join the class, be sure you clarify what kind of course this is:

- a course in how to study the Bible
- a course that requires homework
- a course that will challenge them to become students.

View your learners as tender plants. Until they get some roots down, they may die on you. Many persons have so seldom been involved in analyzing a Bible passage on their own that they become frightened and frustrated. They don't have confidence in the potentials of their own minds to learn these skills. You have to nurture them tenderly with encouragement and consideration through the first sessions until they can discover their own capabilities.

The persons who may have the most trouble with comprehending the skills will be those who have had little Bible background, who are limited in grammatical knowledge, who do little reading, who are used to being "spoon-fed," who are "motor" people, enjoying physical work more than analyzing literature.

The persons who will be the most enthusiastic are those who want to learn how to study on their own, who are tired of being "spoon-fed," who are analytical in their minds, who want to go deeper in Bible study, who are educators, recognizing the process as sound educational approach to study. But there is no one who will not benefit somewhat from the course, even though they invest very little in it. All will find that the skills do help them in reading their Bibles with greater perception.

Setting

You are to teach this course in a room where you have tables. Your students are to sit around tables, three or four at each, but seldom more than four. If there are too many at a table, sharing becomes a problem. All cannot have a turn as often.

They should remain at the same tables for several sessions, learning how to work together as teams. They need several sessions to get to know each other and become free with each other in the sharing. But the groups at the tables could be changed at least midway in your course so they learn how to share with others.

Materials

Textbook: The Joy of Discovery in Bible Study. All your students must have a copy of this book. It is your main "track" and you will pretty much follow the suggestions in it. The suggestions in the *Discovery Skills* sections will be your guide.

Bibles and Resources: You will also need a variety of Bible translations. Possibly your students will bring their own versions. You also should have some other resources such as Bible dictionary, dictionary, and samples of commentaries.

Possible Teaching Sessions

The course is flexible and can be taught in a variety of ways. Note the detailed outline of the sessions on this page and the next.

SHORT COURSE

Phase I—The Discovery Phase can be taught in four two-hour teaching periods or 8 one-hour periods. This short course can be taught to persons interested in gaining a "taste" of how to study the Bible.

LONGER COURSE

This would include teaching both *Phase I—The Discovery Phase* and *Phase II—The Expanding Phase.*

These phases can be taught in 8 two-hour periods or 16 one-hour periods, but 10 two-hour periods or 20 one-hour periods are better. The course can be expanded into a 30-hour course for colleges. The longer the course, the more the persons will develop their skills. It is very much like taking piano lessons, the more a person practices, the more he develops the skills.

Teaching Situations

The course will lend itself to many situations:

- informal home study
- in a series of Sunday morning sessions
- in a series of evening sessions
- in a workshop of varying lengths
- in a college or seminary course of 20 to 30 hours.

Outline of Sessions

PHASE 1 — The Discovery Phase

A. Introduction to Process (*Joy of Discovery*, Chapters 1, 2)
B. Use of Tools (JOY, Chapter 2)
C. Observing a Narrative (JOY, Chapter 5: Practice A, 1, 2)
D. Interpreting a Narrative (JOY, 5: B, C)
E. Learning to See (JOY, 3:A)
F. Interpreting Matthew 6:25-34 (JOY, 3:B)
G. Personalizing Matthew 6:25-34 (JOY, 3:C)
H. Increasing Your Skills—1 Cor. 13 (JOY, 4:A)
I. Interpreting 1 Cor. 13 (JOY, 4:B)
J. Personalizing 1 Cor. 13 (JOY, 4:C)
K. Response to the Word (JOY, pp. 38-39)

PHASE 2 — The Expanding Phase

L. Studying a Book (JOY, 7:A)

M. Observing James 3:6-12 (JOY, 7:B)

N. Observing James 3:1-5 (JOY, 7: p. 56)

O. Interpreting James 3:1-12 (JOY, pp. 53, 54, 56)

P. Expressing Creatively (JOY, pp. 55, 57)

Q. Observing the Whole (JOY, 8:A)

R. Interpreting James 3:13-18 (JOY, 8:B, C)

S. Summarizing Through Charts (JOY, 9:B)

T. Analyzing One Paragraph (JOY, 9: page 67)

U. More About Interpretation (JOY, 10:A, B)

V. More About Charts—James 4-5 (JOY, 11: pp. 77, 78)

W. Meditation—James 4-5 (JOY,11: p. 79)

X. Analyzing James 4:7-10 (JOY, 11, pp. 78, 79)

Y. Analyzing James 5:13-16 (JOY, 11, p. 80)

Z. Book Chart (JOY, p. 80)

AA. Theme Study (JOY, p. 81)

BB. Team Project (JOY, p. 81)

CC. Evaluation (JOY, p. 81)

Arrangement of Sessions

1. For an 8-hour series:
   1st hour: Sessions A-B
   2nd hour: Session C
   3rd hour: Session D
   4th hour: Session E
   5th hour: Sessions F-G
   6th hour: Session H
   7th hour: Sessions I-J
   8th hour: Session K

2. For a 16-hour series:

1: A-B	9: N
2: C	10: O
3: D	11: P
4: E	12: Q-R
5: F-G	13: S-T
6: H	14: U
7: I-J	15: W
8: L-M	16: CC

3. For a 20-hour series:

1: A-B	11: P
2: C	12: Q-R
3: D	13: S
4: E	14: T
5: F-G	15: U
6: H	16: V
7: I-J	17: W
8: L-M	18: Y
9: N	19: Z
10: O	20: CC

4. For a 30-hour series:
   Use all the sessions

Guidelines for the Sessions

Use of Guidelines

On the following pages are detailed guidelines for teaching this course. I have tried to indicate how to handle the activities in a one- and a two-hour teaching period. It is impossible to provide detailed instructions for all the ways this course might be taught. My hope is that these guidelines will provide direction for you in planning your own sessions, making the changes you need to best fit your situation.

Importance of Process

Because this is a course on skills, the process is more important than the end product. In the sessions your participants will be introduced to new skills, then practice them a little, but continue with the practice outside the session. But there will not be time for them to perfect any skills during the course. Hopefully they will gain insight, but they will not "arrive" during the course. As leader, your task is to introduce them to the skills and involve them enough in the practice so they learn the basics. The rest they will have to develop on their own.

Every session must have three parts to it.

Part 1. The students share with each other in their teams their insights gained in their home study.

Part 2. The students share a few of their insights with entire group.

Part 3. The leader introduces the new skills for their home study. Your participants will get very little out of the course unless they do some home study, but they must be prepared for their home study.

Importance of Time

Time will always be a problem in conducting the sessions. You will never have time to do everything. In all of these three aspects, you have to watch your time diligently and cut all discussions shorter than your participants will want them cut. But you have no choice. It will never be possible to focus on all the teachings in the passage they are studying. Many "goodies" in a passage will have to be ignored or barely referred to. At times you will be distressed over the fact that "the students are not getting all they should from a passage." You will be tempted to spend another session just studying a passage. You can do this if you have unlimited sessions for teaching the course, but not if you have a limited number.

The important thing is the process and not the grasp of the content of a passage. Some other time they can study the passage in more depth. Now they are learning the skills in how to study a passage in depth. You have to keep reminding the students of the purpose of the course too, because they will often want to do a more thorough study of each passage.

Use of *The Joy of Discovery* with "leaderless" groups

Possibly you are one of several persons who want to study the suggestions in *The Joy of Discovery,* but you have no leader. None of you have been involved in the skills described in the book, but you want to learn the skills on your own. These guidelines should provide direction for your sessions together. They will give you some idea as to what to do together in your sessions and what your home study should be. If you are a very small group, you can be very free in how much time you spend on each skill.

Additions to Guidelines

Because of lack of space, several things are omitted in the guidelines: specific objectives for each session; opening devotions; closing prayer times. The focus described in each session reflects the objectives. You as leader can add your own opening and closing devotions. I encourage you to involve your students in times of prayer. While the emphasis may be on skills, your students will become very much involved in the personal aspects of the Bible teachings. As they learn to know each other, they will become more free and open in the sharing of problems and concerns and will welcome opportunities for prayer.

Time Suggestions

In order to help you allocate your time, suggestions are made for each activity in the session. The purpose of these is to show you the approximate time you might allow for each activity. You may spend a much shorter time on some and longer on others, but use the suggestions as guides. They indicate which activities need the most time.

Introducing the Study

FOCUS

The focus of this first session will be on getting acquainted with each other and with the course: its purpose, the basic procedures in Bible study, the tools needed. Your first session is crucial in that many of your students may not know what to expect. They may become a little frightened when they begin to realize how much personal involvement there will be. Recognize this possibility. Try to establish a relationship of relaxed informality between you and your students. Help them view themselves as persons with great potential.

PROCEDURES

1. Introduce the participants. (15 minutes)

Have the participants introduce themselves to each other around their tables. If they do not know each other, have them share names and some facts about themselves. If they do know each other, have them share their expectations for the course.

Then have them share some things with entire group.

Place a continuum on the board and have them rank themselves in terms of their experience with Bible study, selecting one of the numbers. Take a poll by having them raise their hands.

very little study   1   2   3   4   5   6   very much study

2. Introduce the course. (10 minutes)

Explain that the course is on methods in Bible study. Introduce the title of the course: *The Joy of Discovery in Bible Study*. Explain that the purpose of the course is to introduce to them the skills which will enable them to discover the teachings in Scripture. They will be involved in experiences which will help them learn to study their Bibles with greater insight and awareness. They will be involved in "discovery skills" which will help them learn how to discover the truths in the Bible.

Have the following quotation printed on a large sheet of paper.

> It is only when truth is discovered
>   that it is appropriated.
> When a man is simply told the truth,
>   it remains external to him,
>   and he can quite easily forget it.
> When he is led to discover the truth himself,
>   it becomes an integral part of him
>   and he never forgets.
>   —Barclay

Have them select the key words in the quotation.

Have them discuss meaning of some of the key words: *discover, appropriate, external, integral.*

Evaluate the quotation. Do they agree or disagree with it? Why?

Explain that this quotation reflects the purpose of the course, to help them become discoverers.

3. Introduce the resource book. (5 minutes)

Give each participant one of the books, *The Joy of Discovery in Bible Study.*

Have them note the *table of contents* and the titles to the chapters. Explain that the titles reveal the emphasis in each chapter, reflecting the kind of skills they will be learning.

Explain that the purpose of this book is to help persons become "discoverers" in Bible study and find joy in the process. Explain that the rationale for what is included in this book is found in the quotation which they have just discussed: when persons learn how to discover biblical truths for themselves, they will remember the truths much longer and they will have much more influence and meaning for their lives.

4. Introduce general procedures in Bible study. (10 minutes)

Explain that they are to read these chapters carefully after class, but now they will look at some of the general procedures in Bible study. Have them turn to page 14 and note the chart.

Ask them to recall the steps in their study of the quotation. Which of these steps did they follow? They will discover they did most of them.

Explain that these are the steps they will follow in learning how to study the Bible, but that they are also steps which persons must follow in all study. We follow these steps even when reading the daily newspaper.

Have them read the brief description of each in the left column and just scan what is said in the right column. You may have them underline the key word in the brief descriptions, such as underlining *exactly* in the first one, etc. Also it might help their understanding if they added a question in each section which further describes the process.

1. What does it say?
2. What does it mean?
3. What is the big idea?
4. What is its value for today?
5. What does it mean to me?
6. What shall I do?

5. Discuss tools for Bible study. (10 minutes)

Have them note the kinds of tools a person might have for studying. You should have samples of some of the Bible translations. Help them know the difference between a standard version and the free translations and paraphrases. Encourage them to do their basic study with a standard version and use the others for enrichment and interpretation.

6. Suggest home study or have a break. (10 minutes)

What you do at the end of this session depends on whether you are conducting one-hour or two-hour periods. If your students have only a one-hour period, then you will suggest home study before they go. The home study will always be a shorter one for those in the one-hour period than for those in two-hour periods because they have to prepare for only one hour. The two-hour persons have to prepare for two hours.

Beware of scaring your students with the suggested home study. Describe the home study as open-ended. They should try to do as much as possible. Identify with their problems of doing homework, as persons who are busy in business, home, etc. Yet this course is like a typing class, the more they practice the more they will learn.

For the one-hour students:

a. Read Chapters 1, 2, 5, 14 in *The Joy of Discovery*. While they are to read Chaper 5, they are not to do the Bible study. Encourage them to underline what they consider as significant statements.

SESSION B.

Use of Tools

If you are having 30 sessions, spend another session on tools and translations.

SESSION C.

Observing a Narrative
FOCUS

The focus in this second session will be mainly on observing, although persons are always involved in the entire process: observing, interpreting, summarizing, personalizing.

You will notice that we begin with Chaper 5 in *Joy of Discovery*. They will first learn how to use these six guide words *(where, when, who, what, why, how)* as a means for increasing their powers of observation.

At first I had students begin with the suggestions in Chapters 3 and 4. But I found that the approaches in Chapters 3 and 4 were more difficult and created some frustration. In the beginning it is important for students to be involved in activities which provide the most satisfaction and the least frustration. The suggestions in Chapter 5 have these qualifications. You are most apt to lose your students in the first two sessions if they develop the feeling that the approaches are too difficult for them. Always remember that you are nurturing tender plants. Keep encouraging them. Of course you will have some "sturdy oaks" who do not need as much encouragement, but they are seldom in the majority.

PROCEDURES

1. Discuss importance of observation. (10 minutes)

Have your students recall the six procedures in Bible study (page 14 in *Joy of Discovery*). Write them on the chalk board. Review their meanings. Circle step one, *Observation*.

Explain that observation is the first and most important step in the process. If a person does not observe carefully and accurately, he will not be able to interpret and apply fairly. At first most persons are not careful observers. To learn to observe exactly what an author is saying is like any other skill. It takes time and practice. Most of us do not know how to observe because we do not know what to look for. One purpose of this course is to teach them some clues, some things to look for which will increase their powers of observation.

Have your students look at the titles of Chapters 3, 4, and 5 in *Joy of Discovery*. Explain that the purpose of all three chapters is to help them learn how to observe. Admit that it is not easy to learn how to observe all of the details in a passage. The question is, where to begin? What is the easiest way to teach persons to observe?

We need to begin with the simplest steps because persons can become discouraged if they have difficulty with observation. Explain that at first students used to begin with the suggestions in chapters 3 and 4. But because these suggestions are more difficult, it seems the best place to start is with the suggestions in chapter 5. These seem to be the simplest steps for a beginning student.

2. Study Chapter 5 in Joy of Discovery. (5 minutes)

Have them turn to Chapter 5 and note the six guide words: *where, when, who, what, how, why*. Discuss their meanings. Explain that these six words are especially helpful for studying a narrative, but can be used with any passage. They are always helpful in observing the details in a passage. Also discuss the three approaches to a narrative.

3. Focus on observation of Luke 23:32-49. (15 minutes)

Explain the purpose of the *Discovery Skills* section in each chapter: to provide practice exercises for them to learn the skills in Bible study.

a) *Practice A:1:* Do this practice exercise together. Read one paragraph at the time and have them look for the *where, when, who, what* in each one. Do this quickly because they will study the passage in detail in the next exercise.

b) *Practice A:2:* Have them divide a sheet of paper in four parts and title them as is suggested on page 35 in the textbook. Explain that by writing down some of their observations they will get deeper insights into what the passage is saying. Note that they are to begin with v. 34, not with v. 32. Work with them on v. 34. 1) In the *Who* column, write *Jesus;* 2) in the *How Jesus responded* column, write *Jesus' words;* 3) in the *Who* column, write *they;* 4) in the *What they did* column, write *cast lots to divide garments.* The question may come as to who are the *they.* A cross reference (Mark 15:16) will reveal the *they* are the soldiers.

Have them continue the study on their own. If you feel that they are still troubled, do v. 35 together also.

After most of them seem to have completed the exercise, have them share what they wrote down. Some may still be puzzled about in which column they should have written things. Tell them that where they placed the observations was not as important as what they observed. The purpose of the exercise was to sharpen their powers of observation. Ask them in what way they gained more insight into the story by doing this exercise.

4. Focus on interpretations. (15 minutes)

Refer to the list of procedures you have on your chalk board. Have them note that the second step in the study is *interpretation.* To interpret is to seek to know meanings. Have them note on p. 36 in the textbook the ways we can interpret passages: *build mental images; ask questions; answer questions by defining words, using cross references, comparing translations, consulting other resources.*

a. *Practice B:1—Build mental images:* Have them try to imagine what it was like to be at this scene. Assign groups of people to different tables: the *rulers,* the *soldiers,* the *criminals,* Jesus' *friends,* the *centurion.* Have them try to imagine if they had been one of these persons, what they would see, hear and how they would feel. Let them share with each other, and then report to the entire group. Encourage them to speak in first person, "If I were the centurion I would feel . . . . "

b. *Practice B:2—Ask yourself questions:* Explain that asking questions is a very important aspect of Bible study. Since they have not had any practice in asking questions, some questions are provided for them. Have them note the questions. Invite them to think of other questions which they might ask to gain deeper insight into the story.

c. *Practice B:3—Seek to find answers to questions:* Have them note the different ways they might answer some of the questions.

5. Suggest home study. (10 minutes)

Emphasize the importance of home study. Because this is a skills course, only as they do some practice at home will they get very much out of the course. Also remind them that this is a team-learning course. Much that they learn will be from each other as they share their home study. Since some may get frightened about the prospects of home study, try to assure them that they will not be graded on their home work, but that no matter what they do and share, it will be a blessing to others.

For those in two-hour period:

a. *Practice B:2-3* Have the students try to answer the questions by following some of the suggestions in B:3, p. 36.

b. *Practice C:2 Identify with a person* Have them select one of the statements which best reflects their response to Jesus right now in terms of some situation.

c. Read Chapters 1, 2, 3, and 14 in *Joy of Discovery.*

For those in one-hour period:

a and *b* as described above.

Reminder: Call your students before the next session to see how they are getting along with the home study. This is one way to encourage them in doing some of the home study.

It is very important that you do all of the assignments which you give to your students. One of the reasons is to be appreciative of any of the problems which they may have in the study. Another is so that you may be able to add to what they give. While your students are to be the first "contributors," their observations and interpretations may not be very thorough at first. You need to make a very thorough study of each passage so that you can quickly add to their suggestions, point out observations which they may have missed, highlight key questions, briefly interpret any difficult passage.

Interpreting a Narrative

FOCUS

The focus in this session is mainly on interpreting and personalizing the teachings in Luke 23:32-49. Also you might discuss the value of team learning. One part of their home study was to read Chapter 14, "Discovery with Others," in *Joy of Discovery*. Group sharing is very important in the learning process. When persons realize that they are to share their home study with others, they take the home study more seriously. In group sharing, they not only learn from each other, but they also gain confidence in themselves. As one student said, "It is good to hear what others have discovered in their studies, but it is even better to realize that you discovered some things that they didn't."

PROCEDURES

1. Review. (5 minutes)

In the beginning of each session, encourage students to share their reactions to their home study—feelings, frustrations, joys. If they are having difficulties, you want to hear about them.

2. Discuss value of team learning. (5 minutes)

Spend only a few minutes on this discussion, but invite them to share their reactions to Chapter 14, "Discovering with Others." Have them share the advantages of working together in small groups at the tables. Also discuss what it means to be an enabler. Explain that you as a leader are to be an enabler to them, enabling them to become discoverers. But they also are to be enablers to each other, enabling each other to get as much out of the course as possible. They have the opportunity to bless and be blessed by what each one does.

3. Share personalizations. (15 minutes)

I am suggesting that your students might focus on personalizing the teachings in Luke 23:32-49, before they consider the interpretations, but feel free to begin with either. One part of their assignment was to identify with the feelings of some person at the cross (Practice C:2, page 37). Have them share with their tablemates, which of the responses they selected and Why. Remind them that they are to share a present-day feeling relating to a current situation, not how they would have felt if they had been at the cross.

After the table sharing, invite several to share with the entire group. There is need for some general sharing with the entire group to create cohesiveness among the whole group. If your group is very small, you would have only general sharing.

4. Share interpretations (15 minutes)

Have them share their interpretations with their tablemates first. In order that all have opportunity to share, suggest that each shares *one thing* the first time around. The tendency in some groups is for one person to do all the talking and the rest share just "what is left over."

You will have to cut short the small group sharing in order to have some time for large group sharing. Invite some general sharing in terms of the meaning of Jesus' names and the word "save." You might focus their discussion on some of these questions: What is the meaning of the word *save?* What are some things from which persons need to be saved?

5. Suggest home study or have a break. (5 minutes)

For those in one-hour period:

a. Read Chapter 3 in *The Joy of Discovery*.

Reminder: If you are conducting a two-hour period and if this is the first session in a two-hour period, it would be helpful if you limit the activities suggested in this session to about 45 minutes, allowing a longer time for those in the next session. In Session E your students are introduced to another approach to observation and it takes longer to teach them this approach. The more time you have the better.

DISCUSSION HELPS

One of the clues in this story are the pronouns the soldiers and the rulers used for Jesus. The pronouns themselves reflected action. The soldiers spoke directly to Jesus, coming up to him, offering him vinegar and joking said, "If you . . . . " But the rulers did not speak to him, only to each other. Can we not imagine the rulers nudging each other, tossing their heads toward Jesus, maybe pointing a thumb in his direction as they scoffed, "He saved others, let him save himself if he is the Christ, the Chosen One!"

In the discussion of the word *save,* have the group give you some meanings for the word and what are some things from which persons needed to be saved. A common interpretation of the statement "Jesus saves," is that he saves us from hell after death. The Greek word for save, *sōzein,* means to save in more than a theological sense. It is a word which means rescue from danger, to heal in sickness, to be delivered from danger, from disease, from the condemnation of God, from the power and guilt of sin, from slavery and bondage. I believe that Jesus came to save us from the "here and now" hells as well as the "hereafter" ones. Invite your students to think about the kinds of hells of today from which Jesus can save persons.

SESSION E.

Learning to See

FOCUS

The focus in this session is on the observation skills described in Chapter 3 of *The Joy of Discovery*. This will be their first introduction to observing the many things described in the charts on pages 18 and 19. At first your students may feel overwhelmed with the many things to observe. If grammar is difficult for them, some may feel frustrated and discouraged. Others may feel it is tedious to observe the many details. Most people are shallow in their observations until they begin to look for specific things.

Be certain that *you* have carefully done the observing and asking questions on Matt. 6:25-34 before you can teach this session.

PROCEDURES

1. Introduce ways to observe. (10 minutes)

Explain that they have had one practice in learning how to observe. During this period they are to practice some other ways to develop their powers of observation. They were to read Chapter 3 in *The Joy of Discovery*, so they already have had some introduction to the other approaches.

Discuss the charts on pp. 18-19 in *The Joy of Discovery*. Have them note the main categories as listed in the left column of each chart. Explain that the many categories may seem overwhelming at first, but as they practice, these approaches will become a part of their thinking.

2. Practice observations on Matt. 6:25-34. (10 minutes)

a. *Provide each one with another copy of the passage (Matt. 6:25-34).* Have it typed in the same way as the printed copy in the textbook. The extra copy allows for more writing space. When they first begin to record observations, they need more space for writing than is in the textbook.

b. *Note the suggestions in Practice A:1, p. 20.* Remind them that they have already had one experience in observing, using the guide words, *where, when, who, what, why, how.* They should continue to keep these words in mind as they observe, but now they are going to use other ways. Explain that looking for key words is one of the first things they should do no matter what they read.

c. *Look for key words in Matt. 6:25-34.* Read aloud the passage by sections: 6:25; 26-27; 28-30; 31-34. As you read, have the students underline what they consider key words. Have them share after the reading of each section. Be accepting of all they share. After all of the sections have been read, then have them select what they consider are some of *the* key words in the entire passage (anxious, life, body, food, drink, clothing, kingdom, righteousness).

d. *Look for more details.* Explain that they have just begun to observe the details in the passage. To increase their powers of observation they are to look for some of the other things listed in the charts on pp. 18-19. Work together on Matt. 6:25. Have the verse printed on a large sheet of paper or in the center of the chalkboard. If you have an overhead projector, then use that. In order to help the students learn how to record observations, you are to record on your paper or board as they record on their sheet.

Invite the students to share what they observe. On p. 22 there is a sample of the kinds of things they might observe, but don't have them look at this until after they have done their own observations. Rather suggest that they have their books open to the charts on pp. 18-19. Someone may say that the verse begins with the connective "therefore." Write down whatever observations they give you on your paper or board as they write on theirs. Remind them to keep the right margin open for other use. Don't go into too much detail. Try to make the observations seem simple so persons will not become frightened and think that observing is too difficult for them. Work together only on Matt. 6:25.

3. Practice asking questions. (10 minutes)

Explain that as we observe details, another process usually goes on at the same time. We sometimes ask ourselves questions about the words or phrases which we observe. This is a very important process, because it is the bridge between *observation* and *interpretation.* Remind them that in their first study, the questions were furnished for them. Now they are to begin to ask questions themselves.

Have them read the information about asking questions on pages 22 and 23. Write on the board the clues for asking questions: *Why did Jesus say . . . ? Meaning of . . . ? Significance of . . . ? Implication of . . . ? Relationship between . . . ?* Have them close their books so that they can't copy from the sample given on page 23. As they suggest questions, write them on the board or sheet as they write in the right margin of their sheets. Inform them that they should ask questions about the things they have observed, so their questions should be opposite their observations. Observing and asking questions are processes which they are to do at the same time.

At first you may have to guide them in the kinds of questions to ask. Remind them that the purpose of asking questions is to force ourselves to think seriously about the observations and to discover what ideas need to be interpreted. The asking of questions is the bridge between observation and interpretation. They are not asking these questions for someone else to answer, but for themselves to answer. Admit that they will not always be able to answer all the questions they might ask. Remind them that they are not to answer the questions yet. First, they must observe the entire passage before they try to interpret.

4. Practice observing and asking questions on other sections. (25 minutes)

Divide the sections of Matt. 6:25-34 among your tables: 26-27; 28-30; 31-32; 33-34. If you have more tables than sections, several can have the same. Explain that they are to work together at each table, making *observations* and asking *questions for understanding* concerning the section they have. Mingle among the tables. The students may need some help and encouragement. They may worry about whether they are saying the "right or wrong" things about the words and phrases which they are observing. Help them realize that they are not to evaluate what they do as "right or wrong." Rather they are to realize that "wrestling" with observations and questions is helping them learn to *think* as they read, even if they can't identify everything they see.

After allowing them time to do some observing and questioning, have each table report on their observations and questions. Feel free to add any significant ones they may have omitted.

5. Suggest home study. (5 minutes)

Have your students note the various ways to answer questions on page 23 and 24 in *The Joy of Discovery*. Discuss the various ways. Remind them that not all of the questions a person asks himself might be relevant and worth answering. They need to learn how to select the key ones.

a. *Practice B-2:* They are to try to answer one or two of their key questions, using some of the ways suggested in this practice section. They are to be the interpreters of the section on which they have just focused. The table which worked with 6:26-27 should also work on

6:25. Remind your students that they are responsible for only a few verses, but to feel free to interpret as many as they would like.

b. *Practice C—Personalize Biblical Teachings:* Encourage them to select one of the suggestions for application of teachings.

c. Read Chapter 4, pages 25-28, and Chapters 6 and 13 *(only for those in two-hour session).*

Reminders: Sometimes persons slip in "application questions" when writing the "questions for understanding." Be on the watch for these. An application question will have the pronouns "us" or "we" or "me." ("Why shouldn't *we* be anxious?") Remind your students that when they are asking questions, they are trying to find out *what the author meant* by what he said: What did Jesus mean by what he said . . . ? They can ask application questions, but only after they have tried to interpret the passage.

OBSERVATION HELPS

In the beginning many persons have difficulty making observations and asking questions. It is helpful if you can give them a sample copy of the kinds of observations one can make and the kinds of questions one can ask in relation to the entire passage of Matthew 6:25-34. This would mean that you would have to make a thorough study yourself and then have it duplicated for your students. They will be encouraged when they find their own observations and questions on the copy you give them and will be challenged by seeing what other observations and questions they might have included. You would give them the copy after they had worked on their own in class.

SESSIONS F-G.

Interpreting Matthew 6:25-34

FOCUS

The focus in this session is mainly on interpreting and personalizing the teachings in Matthew 6:25-34. Since their home study centered on these two aspects, the session time should be one of sharing. Remember that your role is that of the *summarizer* and *enricher.* After the students have shared their insights, then add other significant insights which may have been omitted. If you want to extend this session into two, then spend this hour on interpretation and the next on personalization.

PROCEDURES

1. Share reactions. (10 minutes)

Invite the students to share reactions to their home study. Did they have difficulties? Frustrations? You might also have them complete this statement: One thing I have already learned . . . .

2. Share interpretations. (20 minutes)

Have the students share their interpretations with those at their own tables. Again remind them to take turns so all have opportunity to share. Usually the sharing is very animated, and they could continue much longer than you can allow them to share (10 minutes).

Invite each table to select a reporter and share some of the most significant insights about their section of the passage, gained in their study and discussion. When all tables have had opportunity to share, then you may want to discuss some of these questions:

1. What is Jesus really trying to say in this passage?

2. What are ways to combat anxiety?

3. Study structure of Matthew 6:25-34. (10 minutes)

Explain that the structure of a passage is another important thing to observe. Have your students turn to p. 21 in their textbook and consider the structure of Matthew 6:25-34. Ask them how they would bracket the verses in terms of content—which verses seem to focus on the same thing. Place the numbers of the verses in a vertical column on the board and bracket them according to their suggestions. Hopefully they will eventually see that they should be bracketed thus: 6:25; 26-27; 28-30; 31-34. After the bracketing of the verses, then have them summarize each section. The following is a simple summary of the passage but accept the summaries they give you.

> 6:25   General question
>
> 6:26-27 Illustration relating to life
>   God's concern for life
>
> 6:28-30 Illustration relating to body
>   God's concern for body
>
> 6:31-34 Challenge—seek God first

4. Share personalizations. (15 minutes)

Note some of the possibilities on p. 24, *Practice C*. Have them share at their tables or with the entire group. If possible, have a few share a time when they put complete trust in the Lord and he did supply their needs.

5. Suggest Home Study

For those in one-hour session

a. Read Chapters 4, 6, and 13 in *Joy of Discovery.*

Session break for those in two-hour sessions.

SESSION G.

Personalization of Matthew 6:25-34

If you wish to extend the session, spend one hour on personalization.

SESSION H.

Increasing Your Skills

FOCUS

This session focuses on observation of 1 Cor. 13. While this is a familiar passage, your students will be amazed at how much more they will see in the chapter when they carefully observe the details. Some may question the value of observing details and asking questions. They may feel it is tedious to write detailed observations and repetitious to keep asking the same questions. It may seem to them as if they are just asking questions to ask questions. These are normal reactions at first.

Keep reminding them that developing these skills is just like developing any other skills. There is a certain amount of "finger exercises" we have to work on. Help them realize that in the beginning they have to keep on doing what may seem tedious and meaningless. But as they do them, they will more and more discover the value of carefully observing details and asking questions.

PROCEDURES

1. Review the procedures in Bible Study. (10 minutes)

Have them review the six steps in Bible study. As they give them to you, write them on the board. Then have them list some of the ways that can help them to observe, ask questions, and interpret.

Your board should include some of these things:

Six Steps	Observation	Questions for Understanding	Interpretation
observation	key words		define
	admonitions	Why?	translations
interpretation	advice	Meaning of?	cross references
	results	Significance?	resources
summarization	reasons	Implication?	wrestle
	contrasts	Relationship?	
evaluation	comparisons		
	connectives		
application	illustrations		
	guide words		
actualization	etc.		

On page 79 is a chart of the *Methodical Procedures in Bible Study*. If possible, have the chart duplicated for your students and give it to them after this review or use it as the basis for review.

2. Focus on Chapter 4 in The Joy of Discovery. (5 minutes)

Have the group turn to Chapter 4 in *The Joy of Discovery* and note the detailed descriptions concerning the things to observe. You might call special attention to several of the sections, such as 2, 3, 5 and 8. Don't spend too much time on the sections, except for the one on grammar. Admit that grammar is a problem to many persons. Yet observing grammar is important because some of our doctrines are based on grammatical constructions. Assure them that they can learn to observe even if they cannot identify the grammatical construction of words. Encourage them to be observant of the verbs at least.

3. Focus on observations in 1 Cor. 13.

a. *Provide additional copy.* As you did with Matthew 6:25-34, try to provide each person with an additional copy of the passage so that they can make their first observations on this sheet, rather than in their book. Have them turn to p. 29 and note the suggestions in *Practice A.*

b. *Look for key words* (5 minutes). Again remind them that the first step in study is to be on the alert for key words. Since they all know the passage, you might save time by assigning sections to different tables. They are to quickly scan for key words. Sections: 13:1-3; 4-7; 8-10; 11-13. Then have each table share some of their key words. Finally, have them select some of the key words in the entire passage (love, tongues, knowledge, prophecy, faith, child, etc.). If you have a large group, several tables can have the same section.

METHODICAL PROCEDURES IN BIBLE STUDY

Observation	Questions for Understanding	Interpretation	Summarization	Personalization

(Things to look for)
key words
advice-warnings
admonitions
exhortations
cause-effect
reasons
results
promises
questions
illustrations
contrasts
comparisons
repetitions
progressions
grammatical
  construction
  connectives
  pronouns
  nouns
  adverbs
  adjectives
  verbs
where? when?
what? who?
how? why?
emphatic statements
atmosphere
literary form
general structure
	(clue words)
	Why . . .
	Meaning of . . . .
	significance of . . . .
	implication of . . . .
	progression . . . .
	relationship between
	literal-figurative
		(ways to discern
		  meanings)
		Meditate—pray
		Discern
		Define
		Compare translations
		Investigate
		  cross references
		Consult resources
		Wrestle
			(ways to summarize)
			paraphrase
			summary statements
			outline
			charts
			diagrams
				Evaluation
				Purpose of author?
				For whom written?
				General truths—local
				  truths?
				Relation to whole
				  message of Bible?
				Validity of translation?
				
				Application
				What am I to believe?
				What am I to do?
				What do I learn about
				  relationships?
				What is the Good News
				  for me?
				
				Actualization
				Meditate
				Express faith in
				  concrete ways
				Share convictions
				Make commitments
				Pray

c. *Observe other details* (10 minutes). Have them note the suggestions listed on p. 29 under *Practice A:2 Look for Details.* Have them all focus on 13:1 for observation of other details. Read verse 1 and have them share observations. Here are some possible observations. You may have to do some probing to get all of these observations.

> Begins with conditional clause
> First-person pronouns
> Present-tense verb
> Emphasis on two kinds of tongues
> Cause and effect relationships: "If I . . . I am"
> Contrast "but"
> Compares himself to two things
> Irritating sounds

d. *Ask questions* (5 minutes). Remind them that they are to ask questions as they observe. Have them review the kinds of questions they might ask. Record in the right margin, the *Questions for Understanding.* On p. 31 in the text are some of the kinds of questions they might ask. Don't have them look at this sample until they have asked their own questions.

e. *Work on sections* (20 minutes). Explain that each table is to continue with the process, working with the section which they have already focused on when looking for key words: 12:2-3; 4-7; 8-10; 11-13. They are to make observations and ask questions for their section. Encourage them to work together (10 minutes).

After allowing some time to work on their section, have someone at each table share what they have been doing (10 minutes).

4. Suggest home study. (5 minutes)

a. *Practice B-2:* Review the ways to answer questions. Explain that each table is to try to answer several of the key questions which they asked in terms of their section of 1 Cor. 13. The table which focused on 13:2-3 will also take 13:1 for interpretation.

b. Review Chapter 6 in *The Joy of Discovery.*
   Read 1 Cor. 12 for background to 1 Cor. 13. Have them consider these questions:
   - What is the relationship of 1 Cor. 12 to 1 Cor. 13?
   - Why did Paul begin with the conditional clauses?
   - Why did he not begin with the description of love?
   - What is Paul really trying to emphasize in chapter 13?

c. Read Chapter 7 in *The Joy of Discovery* (for those who are studying Phase II also).

NOTE: If you have college students working for credit, you might have them make observations and ask questions on the entire chapter as a part of their assignment. If you plan to spend three hours on the study of 1 Corinthians 13, then you might spend part of the second hour focusing on observations and include interpretations and personalization the third hour.

Interpreting 1 Corinthians 13

FOCUS

The focus in this session is on interpretation and personalization of 1 Cor. 13. One aspect of their assignment was to read Chapter 6, "Ways to Interpret," in *The Joys of Discovery*. While they have already been involved in the process of interpretation, they may need to discuss some of its aspects.

At first some of their frustrations center in the questions they ask and how to answer them. Should they answer all of them? What if you can't find answers for them all? They are apt to think of questions only as something to answer, rather than direction for interpretation.

Help them to realize that the asking of questions is to direct their thinking, but they do not have to answer all of them. Gradually they will learn which are relevant and which are not relevant to the passage. They are to wrestle with only the relevant ones. The purpose of answering a question is to find meaning in the passage they are studying.

PROCEDURES

1. Discuss ways to interpret. (5 minutes)

Have the students review the contents of Chapter 6 in *The Joy of Discovery*. Invite any questions they may have about interpretation. Spend only a few minutes on the discussion of the chapter, but possibly you should focus on these areas: reasons for asking questions; ways to answer them; need for wrestling; how to record interpretations.

2. Share home study. (25 minutes)

Have the students share their interpretations with those at their own tables. They all were to focus on the same verses, so this is a way they can enrich each other's home study (15 minutes).

You may have to cut short their table discussions, so that you can have some general sharing. Each table should select a reporter to share some of the significant insights they gained in their study. Invite some general sharing (10 minutes).

3. Focus on the structure of 1 Cor. 13. (10 minutes)

Explain that to really understand this chapter they need to analyze its structure. Have your students study the structural diagram of the passage on page 30 in their textbook. Place on the chalk board the numbers of the verses in a vertical column. Bracket them accordingly:

1:3; 4-7; 8-10; 11-13. Remind them that they have each studied one of the sections of the chapter. As they consider the structure, have them consider these questions:

- What is the emphasis in each section?
- Why did Paul begin with conditional clauses?
- Why did he not begin with the section on love?
- What is the relationship of this chapter to I Corinthians 12?
- Why does he describe both the positive and negative aspects of love?
- What was Paul really trying to say in this chapter?

These questions are not necessarily to be answered one by one, but use them to challenge the students to think about the reason for the structure of the chapter. Summarize each section.

4. Share personalizations. (15 minutes)

Invite the sudents to share ways in which they have found love to be the "more excellent way" for solving difficult situations.

5. Suggest home study. (5 minutes)

What you suggest for home study for those in a one-hour session depends on the length of your series. If your series is eight sessions of one hour each, then the next session is your final session. You might suggest the following:

a. Read Discovery Skills IV, page 38.

b. *Practice A:1-3:* Have them follow the suggestions in this practice.

SESSION J.

Personalizing 1 Corinthians 13

If you wish to extend this session, spend one hour on personalizing 1 Cor. 13.

DISCUSSION HELPS

1 Cor. 13 is an example of a psychological approach in writing. Paul did not write the chapter so much to teach his readers about love as to challenge their pride in their gifts. It is interesting to note that he gives no admonitions. He is not telling them to show love. He is challenging them to take an inventory of themselves to discern just how they are using their gifts.

If he had begun with admonitions to love, they might have agreed with him. But instead he begins with the conditional clause *if . . .* and then with the contrast "but have not love" . . . and finally with a conclusion. His examples are startling. He begins where his readers are, on the gifts about which they have such pride. By the time he has emphasized "but have not love " five times, his readers should be asking, "What is this love that is so important?"

Then he describes the characteristics of love. He seems to be challenging his readers to take inventory. If they are doing any of these things, they do not have this love, and their gifts may have no value. The gifts which they have are not something in which to have such pride. They are transitory, imperfect, incomplete. Only love is lasting and eternal. Gifts are the tools for building the Body of Christ. Love is the way to use the tools.

The sections of the chapter may be summarized in this way: 1-3: value of love; 4-7: characteristics of love; 8-10: transitory and imperfect quality of gifts; 11-13: superiority of love.

SESSION K.

Response to the Word
FOCUS

The focus in this session is on the suggestions described in *Discovery Skills IV*, pp. 38-39 in the textbook. This is an optional lesson. If you are having a series of only eight sessions, this should be your eighth session. If you are teaching more than 8 but less than 20, I suggest you skip this session.

PROCEDURES
1. Focus on responses to the Word.

Since you are to spend only one hour on the study, you will have to shorten the discussion, but you still can cover all the elements in it.

Have your students note the *purpose of Bible study* as described on p. 38. You might discuss the relationship of the passage which they have studied with this next study.

a. *Practice A:1-2:* Do these suggestions together, sharing as you read the passage.

b. *Practice A:3:* Make a special study of Jesus' interpretation. Divide the illustrations among the tables, each focusing on one of them. Have them follow the suggestions in the book (p. 39). They might have difficulty with the pattern, but tell them it is not so important where they place their observations, but that they place them somewhere. Also they can repeat an observation, placing it in several columns.

c. *Practice B:1-2:* Have them just note the suggestions under *1. Ask questions for understanding,* but have them work on the suggestions in *2. Interpret your questions.* Each table is to continue to focus on the illustration they have already studied. Have them share their insights. Have them discuss some of the questions listed in *Practice B-1, a, b; B-2, c.*

2. Evaluate the course.

Allow some time for evaluating the course. Have them complete one of the statements in *Practice C—Ways to Apply and Actualize* (p. 40). Have them share what they have written.

Then have them share their general reactions to the course. They might complete some of these statements:

Some study skills which I have found most helpful are . . . .

Some frustrations I had are . . . .

Some ways I can use these skills are . . . .

Note: Even if your series is longer than eight sessions, you might still want to involve your students in *Session K*. Because of its emphasis on response to God's Word, this parable is an important one to consider.

If you are continuing in the study, suggest the following Home Study:

1. Read Chapter 7 in *Joy of Discovery*.
2. Read the book of James.

SESSIONS L-M.   **PHASE II—The Expanding Phase**

Studying a Book

FOCUS

This is the first session for *Phase II—The Expanding Phase*. The focus is on "Studying a Book," Chapter 7 in *The Joy of Discovery*. If your series is 20 sessions or less, you may want this session to be the eighth in your series. Note the outline of sessions on page 61.

PROCEDURES

1. Introduce Chapter 7, "Studying a Book." (5 minutes)

Explain to your students that they are now in *Phase II—The Expanding Phase*. They have now been introduced to the basic skills in Bible study. In this phase they will continue to develop the skills with some new ones added. The focus now will be on studying a book, the book of James.

Have your students turn to Chapter 7 of *The Joy of Discovery* and note the key ideas on pp. 48-50. If they have had time to read the chapter, have them share some reactions. If not, then quickly summarize the key thoughts in each of the sections: *observing the whole book, discovering the writer and his purpose, discovering the readers, observing the structure of a book.* Admit that you cannot always discern who the writer and readers are, especially in the Old Testament history books.

2. Focus on book of James. (5 minutes)

Have the students note the suggestions for study in *Practice A:1-4* on page 51 in the textbook. Explain that you gain insight into the author and the readers by the statements he makes and the things he emphasizes. You might do some of these things to help them discover author and readers:

- Read James 1:1. What are some facts they learn about both?
- Read James 1:2-4. What more do they learn about both?
- Read James 1:5-8. What additional information?

From the reading of these verses we note that the writer calls himself *James, a servant of God and Jesus Christ,* and is writing to *the 12 tribes of Dispersion.* From the other things he says, we can assume that the readers are Christian *(my brethren),* are having trials, are in need of wisdom and encouragement. The writer believes that trials have value, believes in the prayer of faith, etc.

If you want to extend this session into two hours, spend one hour on this part and the next hour on James 3:6-12.

3. Focus on James 3:6-12. (15 minutes)

If you want to involve your students in *Practice B—Observe Details of James 3:6-12,* you must allow the bulk of your time for this study. Explain that they will begin their study of James by focusing on one of the paragraphs in the center of the book, 3:6-12. Explain that they begin with this paragraph because it is an easy one to analyze. The purpose is to provide them opportunity to continue to develop their skills in Bible study: observing, asking questions, interpreting, personalizing. If they have been given an Overview Chart, have them review it.

a. *Divide a sheet of paper:* Explain that they will use the same pattern which they used in the study of Matthew 6:25-34 and 1 Corinthians 13, only they will have to write down the Scripture passage. They were provided with the Scripture passages in the other studies. Have them divide a sheet of paper into three equal sections, using the paper horizontally to get as wide sections as possible. As they divide their sheets, you divide a chalkboard or large sheet of paper in three sections. If you have an overhead projector, work with it. You will record on the board as they record on their paper. Title the sections: *Observation; Scripture Passage; Questions for Understanding.*

b. *Record unit of words:* Have your students read James 3:6 and ask them: "What is the first unit of words in this verse?" They should give you, "And the tongue is a fire." (Or some other form depending on the translation.) Write this unit of words in the center section of the board as they write the words on their paper.

c. *Observe units of words:* Then ask them, "What observations do you make about this unit of words?" You should get some of these observations: *key words are tongue and fire; tongue is compared to fire; present-tense verb.* Record the observations in the left section as they give them to you.

d. *Ask questions:* Lead them in the third step, that of asking questions. Invite them to share some "meaning" questions they might ask about their observations. Again you should get such questions as: *Meaning of tongue? of fire? Why is the tongue called a fire? Implication of present-tense verb?*

e. *Continue with other units:* Then have the students give you the next unit of words and write these in the center section. Explain that when they copy Scripture for this kind of detailed study, they should always copy units of thought, but not necessarily an entire verse.

Again they are to make observations and ask questions about the words in this unit. Note p. 54 for the way you might divide the units of thought and the kinds of observations and questions they might record. Do not allow them to look at this sample as they work on the verse.

Continue this process until they have completed the study of James 3:6.

4. Discuss the new approach. (5 minutes)

You may need to discuss the new approach. They are now being challenged to be much more detailed in their study. Some will be ready for this challenge, while others might find it somewhat frustrating. Some might think it is just "Mickey Mouse" stuff. Why this emphasis on all the details?

You need to keep reminding them that they are learning how to think. We learn best by disciplining ourselves to write down our thoughts. When this kind of thinking becomes second nature, then we will not need to do so much writing.

5. Divide the task. (20 minutes)

There are several things which you can do after you have worked together on James 3:6. You might continue to work together. You might have them work by themselves. Or you might give each table a large sheet of newsprint. Assign two verses to each table: 3:7-8; 9-10; 11-12. Have them continue the process on this large sheet of paper, working together as a team, writing the Scripture units in the center section, the observations in the left section, and the questions in the right section. When they have completed their observations, they are to display the sheets so all can see what each table has done. If you have many groups and are short of time, you might assign only one verse to each group.

6. Suggest Home Study. (5 minutes)

What you suggest for home study will depend on how much you have accomplished in your class session and how many sessions in your course. If you have accomplished all the activities described in this session, then you might make the following suggestions for home study:

a. Read the book of James.

b. Review Chapter 7 of *Joy of Discovery*.

c. *Discovery Skills VI* (p. 56) —*Practice A:* Observe James 3:1-5 as they did James 3:6-12. If you did not complete James 3:6-12, continue with this study also.

d. If you have only 16 sessions in your series, you may want to compress this study into a shorter period of time. If so, you will add to the assignment:

Practice B, Seek to Know Meanings (p. 56): Have your students interpret one or two verses in James 3:1-12. Assign two verses to each table or group of persons so all verses will be analyzed: James 3:1-2; 3-4; 5-6; 7-8; 9-10; 11-12.

NOTE: If you have college students, you may assign them three or four verses for interpretation, but not the entire passage. In the beginning it is better if they concentrate only on a few verses and do a more thorough job of interpreting. If they have too many verses, they are tempted to be less thorough in their interpreting.

OTHER POSSIBILITIES

If you are having 30 sessions in your series, you may wish to spend one hour on each of these sessions: Session L, Studying a Book; Session M, Observing James 3:6-12.

SESSION L.

Studying a Book

You could spend more time studying an overview of the book of James. You might divide the five chapters with your tables, giving one chapter to each. Have them list the things they learn about the author in one column and the things they learn about the readers in another column. Then have them share their insights. At the close of the period you would introduce the study of James 3:6-12, doing in class only James 3:6.

Observing James 3:6-12

In this session, you would discuss their observations and questions of James 3:6-12 and have them begin a study of James 3:1-5. Their assignment would be to complete the study of James 3:1-5.

Observing James 3:1-5
FOCUS

The focus in this session is on the observations the students have made of James 3:1-12. If you have already had a session on James 3:6-12, then your focus will be only on James 3:1-5. The suggestions described in this session focus on both paragraphs.

PROCEDURES
1. Share observations of James 3:1-12.

Assign the verses in James 3:1-12 to the different tables, giving each two verses: 3:1-2; 3-4; 5-6; 7-8; 9-10; 11-12. If you have already completed the study of James 3:6-12, then assign each table only one verse of James 3:1-5. Have them share their observations with each other. Then share with the entire group.

2. Suggest home study.

Have them review the suggestions for interpretation in *Practice C,* p. 53 in the textbook. Have each table interpret two verses: 3:1-2; 3-4; 5-6; 7-8; 9-10; 11-12.

Those in a two-hour period may not have any time to prepare for their interpretations. You will have to allow them some time during the next session.

Resource Persons: If your students do not have access to many resource books, you might have one or two serve as resource persons each time. They would have the special responsibility of consulting resource books to gain additional insight into a passage. You may have to provide the resource books. Some may want to purchase a commentary on the book of James.

Interpreting James 3:1-12
FOCUS

The focus in this session is on interpreting James 3:1-12. If your students have been involved in the activities described in Session N, then they are ready for interpreting the passage. If they have not shared observations of all of James 3:1-12, you need to provide a little time in the beginning for this.

If you are conducting two-hour periods, this session may come during the second half of the two-hour period. If so, your students will not have time to do any previous study, but will have to interpret what they can through comparing translations, studying cross-references, and wrestling with ideas. You may have to provide background information for some of the statements in the verses.

PROCEDURES

1. Share observations. (15 minutes)

If your assignment included both the observation of James 3:1-5 and the interpretation of two verses in James 3:1-12, invite your students to share their observations of 3:1-5. Possibly you could call for volunteers to share observations, each sharing for one verse.

2. Share interpretations. (40 minutes)

Each table was assigned two verses for special study. Allow them time to share with each other the insights gained in their home study. If some who have not had opportunity for home study, you might supply them with some resources or suggestions.

Invite each table to share some of their key interpretations. They need to be selective, because there is seldom time for students to share all the insights gained through study. Feel free to add your own insights for any part of the passage which may need clarification. If there is time, discuss these questions: What is the significance of the present-tense verbs? Does the tongue always have the potential of being fire? What can control the tongue?

3. Suggest Home Study. (5 minutes)

Practice D—Application (page 55): Have the students complete one of the statements.

Practice C—Creative Expression (page 57): Encourage each person to bring some expression which reflects some insight they have gained in the study of James 3:1-12. If someone feels that he is not very "creative," then suggest he bring a hymn or meditation someone else has written. Emphasize that creativity does not have to do with talent. All persons have creativity, the ability to do something on their own. All persons have inner potentials which they are not developing. Encourage them to develop their potentials.

NOTE for those in a two-hour period: It is possible that *Session P, Expressing Creativity,* may logically come during the second half of a two-hour period. If this happens, your students will not have time to prepare anything creatively. Do not deny them this challenge for expressing themselves in some creative way. Rather, interchange *Session P* and *Session Q, Observing the Whole*. Then the above assignment would be given at the close of Session Q.

SESSION P.

Expressing Creatively

FOCUS

Your students are to share their creative expressions during this hour. Usually when students are challenged to be creative they discover potentials within themselves they did not know they had. The sharing can be a blessing to all.

PROCEDURES

1. Share creative expressions.

If you have a large group, first have them share their contributions with the members of their table. Then they might select one or two to share with the entire group. If you have a smaller group, then have all share with the whole group. Also have them share how they completed some of the statements on p. 55 in the textbook.

2. Suggestions for home study.

Read Chapter 8, "Observing the Whole, in *The Joy of Discovery*.

SESSIONS Q-R.

Observing the Whole

FOCUS

The focus in this session is on "observing the whole," with special emphasis on the "structural diagram." You are introducing to your students one of the most valuable skills in Bible study.

PROCEDURES

1. Focus on Chapter 8 in The Joy of Discovery. (10 minutes)

Have the students turn to chapter 8, "Observing the Whole," in *The Joy of Discovery*. Your students may or may not have read the chapter, depending on the arrangement of your sessions. Briefly summarize the content of the paragraphs on pp. 58 and 59. Discuss the meaning of "structural diagram." Have them turn to pp. 21 and 30 in the text and note the structural diagrams of Matt. 6:25-34 and 1 Cor. 13.

Also have them turn to page 62 and note the structural diagram of James 3:1-12. As they study this diagram, have them identify some of the characteristics. How does it differ from the way it was printed in the Bible? Emphasize the value of learning how to make a structural diagram of a passage. It is the easiest way to analyze a passage.

2. Analyze diagram of James 3:1-12. (5 minutes)

Have the students quickly analyze the diagram of James 3:1-12. Note the suggestions in Practice A:1, p. 61.

3. Make a structural diagram. (40 minutes)

Have the students note the suggestions in *Practice A:2,3*. Have each make a diagram of James 3:13-18 on a sheet of paper. If there is time, then give each table a large sheet of paper and have each table make a diagram of James 3:13-18. Have them analyze their verses, bracketing those which seem to be on the same topic (20 minutes).

Display these so all can see the various ways one might make a structural diagram.

Emphasize that there are many ways to make a structural diagram. The purpose of the diagram is to help persons gain a clearer picture of the content of a paragraph or chapter. They should feel free to set up the structural diagram in any way which best helps them gain insight into the passage.

4. Suggestion for home study. (5 minutes)

Your suggestions for home study will depend on whether you are combining sessions Q and R or treating them separately. If you are short of time you may have to skip *Session R, Analyzing James 3:13-18*. If you plan to include *Session R* in your series, then this might be the home study:

a. *Practice A:2,3:* Analyze James 3:13-18.

b. *Practice B:* Assign one or two verses to each person for interpretation (p. 61).

c. *Practice C:* Meditate on one of the suggestions in this section (p. 63).

SESSION R.
Analyzing James 3:13-18

In this session your students would share their insights gained through their study. The following suggestions might be made for home study:

a. Read Chapter 9 in *Joy of Discovery*.

b. Read James 1.

Summarizing Through Charts

FOCUS

The focus in this session is on the use of charts in studying a passage. The emphasis is on the value of using a chart when trying to summarize the content of a passage.

PROCEDURES

1. Focus on kinds of charts. (5 minutes)

Have your students note the kind of charts shown on p. 66 in the textbook. Have them note the difference between the vertical and the horizontal charts.

2. Analyze structure of James 3. (5 minutes)

Place a vertical chart on the board and divide it into three sections, one for each paragraph in James 3. Have the students quickly summarize the key points in each paragraph. Write these points in each section. Then have them summarize each paragraph with a phrase. Discuss the questions: What is the relationship between these three paragraphs: 3:1-5 on teachers; 3:6-12 on the tongue; 3:13-18 on wisdom?

3. Focus on James 1. (5 minutes)

Have your students turn to James 1 in their Bibles, noting the number of paragraphs. Explain that one of the reasons we did not begin our study of James with the first chapter is because of its many paragraphs and many concepts to consider.

Remind them that so far they have copied down all the words in a passage which they studied. This has value when trying to understand a passage, but it does take time and we do not always have the time. We need to learn other ways to record our observations.

One of them is the recording of observations on a horizontal chart.

4. Summarize paragraphs in James 1. (40 minutes)

Draw a horizontal chart on the board containing eight sections as illustrated on p. 66 in the textbook. Explain that they are to summarize the content in each paragraph. Work together on the first section: James 1:1-4. Read the verses. Then have them give you some summary statements relating to the key ideas. Note the example on

p. 67 in the textbook. Also they are to formulate an over-all summary statement for the paragraph. If you feel it would be more helpful, use the statements in the example and then have the students help you make summary statements for 1:5-8.

Then divide the rest of the paragraphs with the different tables. If you have more paragraphs than tables, have only two persons work on a paragraph. Have them make their summaries on large sheets of paper which can be displayed for all to view them.

Have them also note the way the paragraphs might be bracketed and titled.

5. Suggest home study. (5 minutes)

If you are planning to have both Sessions S and T, then make the following suggestions for their home study:

a. Practice C:1-4. Assign one paragraph to each table for a more thorough study. If you have more paragraphs than tables, leave some out or have fewer persons on a paragraph.

SESSION T.

Analyzing one paragraph in James 1

Have the students share their insights for each paragraph, first with each other at the table and then with the entire group. Make the following home study suggestions:

a. Read chapter 10, "More about Interpretation," in the textbook.

b. *Practice A:1, 2, 3*, p. 71: If possible involve the students in these activities during the Session, either at the end of Session S (if you are not going to have Session T) or at the end of Session T. Then suggest *Practice B—Seek to Know Meanings* as their home study. Encourage them to think how they might visualize the relationship between *faith* and *works*.

SESSION U.

More About Interpretation

Involve the students in the suggestions in *Practice A:1, 2, 3* on p. 71 if they have not previously done them. Give each table a large sheet of paper on which the students are to illustrate their understanding of the relationship between *faith* and *works* according to James' teachings. Then have them display and explain their illustrations.

Home Study

Have them read Chapter 11, "More about Charts and Summarization." If possible, introduce the chapter at the close of the period. Encourage them to make a vertical chart of James 4 or 5. (Practice A, pp. 78 and 80.)

SESSION V.

More About Charts

Have them share their charts of either James 4 or 5. Possibly you might assign one paragraph in either James 4 or 5 to each table to summarize. The class then would make a composite chart of both chapters. Discuss the value of summarizing on charts.

Home Study

Practice C:3 (p. 79). They are to prayerfully meditate on chapters 4 and 5, keeping in mind the questions listed on p. 79.

SESSION W.

Meditation

First have them share their experiences with their meditations.

Home Study

Practice A:3 (p. 80). Make a special study of James 5:13-16.

SESSIONS X, Y, Z, AA, BB.

Note the outline of the session on p. 61 for titles of these sessions and where you can find suggestions for activities. You will include as many as you have time to do. Possibly you will want to spend longer time on some of the other sessions and less time on these topics.

SESSION CC.

Evaluation

Be sure that in your final session you allow time for general sharing of their reactions to the course and for group prayer.

CHAPTER 12

Evaluating
Your Teaching

Evaluating is a natural process. If you have been reading the suggestions in this book, you have been evaluating them in terms of their potentials. If you have been trying some of them, you have been evaluating them in terms of their effectiveness. Evaluating is a necessary process if we desire to increase our effectiveness as teachers. But evaluating can be a discouraging process. Sometimes as we reflect on a teaching session, we *feel* that it was "not good—things went bad." While we are able to identify our feelings of disappointment, we cannot always identify the reason why "things were bad." We don't have definite criteria by which to judge our teaching.

While there are many ways to evaluate the effectiveness of teaching, I shall suggest just three questions which you might use to help you analyze your teaching. These questions will not solve all of your problems, but they may give you direction for evaluation.

What did I LEARN through this teaching session?

As teachers our foremost concern usually is on learning—the learning of our students. Very often we are disappointed in a session because we feel that our students *did not learn* what we hoped they would learn. I am suggesting that you begin with your own learnings: What did you *learn* through this session, not in terms of subject matter but in terms of the teaching-learning process. No matter how disappointing a teaching session might be, it can still be a valuable learning experience for you the teacher. Ask yourself these questions: What did I learn:

- About timing: Did I try to cover too much in the session?
- About focus and purpose: How clear in my own mind were the main concepts and purposes?
- About organization: How carefully planned was my organization?
- About process: What kind of responses did the activities stimulate in my students? What might I do differently?
- About relationships: Was I as concerned about relationships as about content?

As you analyze your teaching, don't think in terms of "good or bad," but in terms of effectiveness. Every session will have some degree of effectiveness. Your purpose for evaluating is to try to identify those things which seemed to increase the effectiveness of your session and those which limited it. Remember that a teacher must have a *barrel* and a *basket*. Into the barrel goes those things which seemed to have the potential for effectiveness. Into the wastebasket goes those things which seemed to hinder the learning process.

How did my learners FEEL about the teaching session?

Note that the emphasis in this question is on the *feelings* of the learner. Indeed we should be concerned about the *learnings* of our students, but we need to be equally concerned about their *feelings*, because their feelings very often color their learnings. Most of us who teach devise ways to gain insight into the knowledge of our students, but few of us really want to know about their feelings. Yet if we really are interested in the learning of our students, we need to provide ways for them to reveal to us their feelings as well as knowledge.

How does the Lord evaluate our teaching?

Fortunately our way of evaluating and the Lord's way are very different. While we are apt to focus on results, his focus is on our motives, our concerns, our hopes, our prayers.

REMEMBER God's promise.

"For as the rain and the snow come down from heaven, and return not thither but water the earth, making it bring forth and sprout, giving seed to the sower and bread to the eater, so shall my word be that goes forth from my mouth; it shall not return to me empty, but it shall accomplish that which I purpose, and prosper in the thing for which I sent it" (Isaiah 55:10, 11).

REMEMBER God's way of working.

"I planted, Apollos watered, but God gave the growth. So neither he who plants nor he who waters is anything, but only God who gives the growth. He who plants and he who waters are equal, and each shall receive his wages according to his labor. For we are God's fellow workers; you are God's field, God's building" (1 Cor. 3:6-9).